ONE MAN'S SEARCH FOR THE SOUL
WITH HELP FROM AN INSIDE SOURCE

SOUL UNDERSTANDING

JOHN DYER

Soul Understanding

This book was printed in the United States of America.

Book Cover Design and Interior Formatting by 100Covers.

ISBN (Paperback): 979-8-9868842-0-2
ISBN (eBook): 979-8-9868842-1-9

CONTENTS

DEDICATION

To my father, who was always there for me. I know now how important that is.

And special thanks to my Muse. I couldn't have done it without you.

DISCLAIMER

This book provides opinions on the subject matter covered. The author is not a Psychologist and is not engaged in rendering psychological or other professional services. If expert assistance or counseling is needed, one should seek the services of a competent professional.

"If in fact we are souls with bodies, rather than bodies with souls, then all souls live on after what we call death, in an invisible dimension. When you are able to make contact with those souls in your dreams, and experience how real they still are, you will see that aging and death are only realities for the five-sensory world. Then ask yourself why you put so much faith in those senses."

—Dr. Wayne Dyer, 1999

"Death is a process of clarification, not liquidation, the purging of your perception of everything but love. Think of your passing as the universe's way of cleaning out your internal closet. The only thing death really takes from you is your clutter."

—Dr. Wayne Dyer
(1 month after his passing)

MY 3 A.M. WAKE-UP CALLS

JUNE 1, 2015

IT'S 3 A.M., and I wake up as usual, with ideas in my head that want me to tell their story.

I reach over to my nightstand and flick on the lamp, then open the nightstand drawer and grab my pen and notepad. I move quickly back to the bed with them. I'm not rushing, but I'm not taking my time either. Past experience has shown me that I don't have much time. The ideas echoing through my head are like thunder rolling across the sky after a lightning strike. Clear now, they will soon fade to silence, never to return.

I have to get them down on paper before they do.

I push a pillow to the headboard and sit up against it. I cross my legs, open the notepad, and rest it on my lap. I take a quick moment to check my posture: back straight, arms loose, neck in alignment with my spine. All is good. I click open the pen and set it to paper. Immediately, it takes off across the page:

Our fears are all different. Our love is all the same.

We don't show our beauty, we shine it.

Only by reaching out to others can we find ourselves.

I write quickly, like a secretary taking dictation from someone who speaks very fast. This has been my calling for the last six months, my obsession really, capturing the ideas that arrive in my head each morning, gathering them on paper for a purpose I do not know. I call these nightly visitations my 3 a.m. wake-up calls, and though I don't know why I am experiencing them, I do know that I am not experiencing them alone. Someone else is receiving these same nocturnal transmissions. The same ideas that are echoing through my head are echoing through his.

My uncle, Dr. Wayne Dyer: self-development author, motivational speaker, spiritual guru. I've felt Wayne's presence often over the last six months, from the moment I began working on a project to optimize his website. This process, known as Search Engine Optimization, involves matching a website's content with the words and phrases that people type into search engines like Google and Bing. Search Engine Optimization is what I do for a living. To do it effectively, I have to understand the message my clients are trying to convey.

This requires research, which in my uncle's case, is no small task. He's written forty-one books throughout his career, many of them bestsellers. Over the past six months, I'd read most of those books. As I did, I compiled a list of topics that his followers were likely to search for Online:

self-development, spirituality, meditation, mindfulness, higher consciousness. This is routine for me, the same procedure I go through with any client. The subject I'm researching doesn't matter to me. My job is to match the content of the client's website with the phrases people are searching for Online.

Except on this project, the subject *did* matter to me. I realized this right away. As I read Wayne's books, I felt a shift taking place inside me, one which I didn't ask for nor expected. Three decades earlier, Wayne underwent a similar shift. He wrote about his experience in a book he called *The Shift*. In it, he described how the focus of his life had changed from "ambition," which he defined as acquiring possessions, power, and status, to "meaning," which he defined as discovering life's true purpose.

> *"I never imagined myself needing to change. I did not have a plan to change my old ways, or a set of goals to improve anything in my life. I felt confident that I had my life running the way I wanted it to. I was extremely successful professionally, and nothing seemed to me to be missing. Yet I have undergone a major transformation that has added a luster to each of my days that I never even contemplated a few years ago."*
>
> —Dr. Wayne Dyer

A similar shift was taking place inside me, as if a higher power had flipped on a light switch inside me. Certainly, I hadn't flipped that switch myself. Like Wayne, I felt that nothing was missing in my life, nor did I plan to change my ways. And yet everything *was* changing about me. My self-concept. My relationship with others. My sense of place in the world.

And my writing. Creative writing, that is. I started writing when I was fifteen, approximately the same age Wayne first set pen to paper. Like him, I would receive ideas at all hours of the day and night. And like him, I would jot those ideas down on scraps of paper that I collected in a grocery bag hidden underneath my bed. But that's where the similarity between us ended. Wayne eventually assembled his notes into a series of successful books. As for me? I stowed my notes on a closet shelf and forgot about them.

It had been twenty years since I'd written anything other than website copy for clients, but now my creativity was flowing again, driven in a new direction by a new-found sense of purpose. I was wading into the current of a whole new stream of ideas. They soaked into me like a dry sponge dipped into a river.

In my head, ideas continue to arrive:

Love that is hoarded is love that is lost.

Empty your closets. Fill your soul.

We go to heaven together. We go to hell one at a time.

The pages fill up quickly, one, two, three, four. At page six, the ideas are done with me, and I stop writing. I tear the written pages from my notepad and take them to my desk, where I number them and staple them together. As a final touch, I add a title to the top of the first page in case I need to refer to this composition later on.

Soaring in Spirit.

Now it's ready to add to the stack.

The stack. That's my name for the knee-high cardboard box that sits under my desk. In that box are hundreds of pages of notes, compositions written on subjects I am largely unfamiliar with: love, forgiveness, faith, power, spirit, fear. The box is three-quarters full already and continues to expand daily. The output of my imagination is overflowing the boundaries of its container, just as the ideas that inspired them are overflowing the boundaries of me.

I add my latest composition to the top of the stack and head back to bed.

At my bedside, I gaze at the box, feeling a combination of wonder and disbelief. The compositions I've collected in there seem alien to me, as if someone else had written them. And yet I also feel attached to them, like a father feels toward his child. This is a new life emerging from me. I'm excited, but also overwhelmed. Like any new father, I feel profoundly unprepared.

I wonder how Wayne will react when I tell him about my shift. One thing I'm sure of is that he won't be surprised. There's always been a deep connection between us, so much so that Wayne once told me that we shared the same mind. I assumed, when he said this, that he was referring to our sense of humor. "Warped minds think alike," I replied in jest. But Wayne saw a deeper bond between us. He believed that our minds were tuned to a different frequency than most people. We could decipher the spiritual transmissions that broadcast through the atmosphere like celestial radio waves.

Everyone senses these transmissions. For most, they arrive as visions, premonitions, intuitions, gut feelings, or déjà vu. But for Wayne and me, these transmissions sparked into words.

It was our shared calling to write these messages down.

Why this calling waited until now to appear, I don't know, any more than Wayne knew why the same calling appeared in him at roughly the same age. I believe that the same higher navigator has been at work inside us, plotting a course for our lives that we could neither conceive nor deny. And so, as I wonder how Wayne will react to the news of my shift, something inside me knows exactly what he will say.

"What the hell took you so long?"

He'll laugh after that, then say, "Tell me all about it. Start from the beginning, and don't leave out a thing."

I look forward to speaking to him about such things. I envision us talking regularly, sharing ideas, maybe even collaborating on a project. But when is the right time to reveal this to him?

It's not today. That much I'm sure of. The ideas are still working themselves out inside me. I need more time to familiarize myself with Wayne's message. And to figure out a message of my own.

I check Wayne's schedule. He's about to embark on a worldwide tour that will end in late August. After that, he'll return home to Hawaii for a short break. I open my calendar and flip through the months. A date quickly catches my eye—September 1. That date holds significance for both of us. Wayne was conceived on that date in 1939. I was born on that date twenty-six years later.

The more I consider my birthday, the more fitting it seems. September 1, 2015. The day my new life will begin.

I feel a surge of excitement as I mark the date on my calendar. Setting a deadline adds a sense of purpose to my task. And a sense of urgency. In three months, I have to figure out what these ideas are adding up to. What I am adding up to.

I climb back into bed, flick off the lamp, and quickly fall back to sleep.

MY SAFE ROUTINE

> *"Because of your formal training you have very likely adopted a skeptical attitude toward spirituality."*
>
> —Dr. Wayne Dyer

MY JOURNEY OF spiritual awakening was neither quick nor easy, and like many, I began by fighting it with all my might.

To say I was a skeptic of spirituality was an understatement. I was the veritable poster child for the too-smart-for-your-own-soul crowd. To help explain this, let me reveal two things about me. First, my mind is like a knife, cold and sharp. Second, until very recently, I took savage pleasure in wielding that knife upon all forms of organized religion.

In hindsight, my wanton assault on the world's sacred cows seems both cynical and pointless to me, but back then I honestly believed I was performing a valuable service to the world. *The road to enlightenment is paved with reason, not faith*. That is what I had been taught, and that is what I believed. The outdated doctrines of the world's hodgepodge of religious traditions stood as obstacles on that road. By removing these obstacles, I was clearing the way for the light of truth to emerge.

That was my hope.

But at some point along my journey, I realized I wasn't progressing anywhere. My spiritual demolition project continued unabated, and yet no light of truth had emerged. By my mid-forties, I found myself in an existential crisis. This globally recognized affliction is known by many names: dukha, melancholy, malaise, the blues. It's a combination of sensations: apathy, frustration, restlessness, fatigue. It's a listlessness you can't seem to awake from, an anxiety you can't seem to shake, an emptiness you can't seem to fill. For me, it felt like I had sprung a pinhole leak, and my life was slowly seeping out of it.

Wayne described the sensation like this:

> *"When you live your life going through the motions, it may seem to be convenient, but the weight of your dissatisfaction creates a huge imbalance in your life. You're perplexed by the ever-present gnawing feeling of dissatisfaction that you can't seem to shake, that pit-of-the-stomach sensation of emptiness. It shows up when you're sound asleep and your dreams are filled with reminders of what you'd love to be, but you wake and return to pursuing your safe routine."*
>
> —Dr. Wayne Dyer

For the last decade, I had gone through the motions and entrenched my safe routine. But my soul continued to whisper to me, imploring me to take a different path. I dealt with my soul's anguish like most people, by pretending it wasn't there. I suppressed it during the day through work, and at night through a few stiff drinks.

A pretty normal existence.

But six months ago, everything changed. Suddenly, my soul wasn't whispering any longer, it was shouting. Its cries seared through my head and coursed through my body. There was nothing I could do but go with the flow.

I continued writing throughout the summer, drawing ever closer to my September 1st deadline. I was tired but happy. For the first time in a long while, I felt like I was headed somewhere rather than just spinning my wheels.

When August 29th arrived, I was ready for my new life to begin. That evening, I wrote a letter to Wayne describing the events of the last nine months. I signed the letter, and then added this postscript:

> A chill comes over me as I sign this letter. In doing so, I am publicly revealing my shift for the first time. The thought of this both excites me and unnerves me. I think I will always remember this day as the turning point in my life. August 29, 2015. The day the new me was born.

I sealed the letter in an overnight envelope and set it on my desk. I would mail it tomorrow so it would arrive on September 1st.

I felt nervous that night, insecure. Something felt off. I told myself this was normal, a simple case of nerves. When you're standing at life's crossroads, facing a new direction, it's always difficult to take the first step.

Eventually, I fell asleep.

No ideas visited me that night.

I woke up the next morning to the news that my uncle had passed away during the night.

TRAGIC LOSS AND MIRACULOUS REEMERGENCE

TO SAY I was devastated doesn't describe it. I was shattered, pulverized, torn inside out. I felt the normal emotions associated with the passing of a loved one: shock, grief, anguish, regret. But my pain had a deeper dimension as well. A darkness fell over me, extinguishing all traces of my newly discovered inner light.

This was a punch to the soul that I didn't see coming, and I wasn't prepared for it at all.

That night, I stared at a photograph of Wayne and me that was taken in Lake Tahoe during a cross-country bike trip he'd encouraged me to do. That was 1981—the year I would start high school, the year Wayne would start an inner transformation that, over the next two decades, would change his life. A new world was opening up for him, one where ordinary rules didn't apply. Here, through an alchemy born of a higher awareness, conflict was transformed into peace, struggle into harmony, problems into miracles. It was a world of real magic, and for the last three decades, Wayne had explored it, chronicling his journey in a series of books, lectures, and television programs. I had discovered this same magical world, and I was hoping to explore it with him. But on the very day my new life was set to begin, his life ended.

On my desk was the overnight envelope I had planned to send him that day. I tore it open and reread my letter. All of it was painful, but one passage particularly so:

> I'm not sure what is happening to me, and I hope you can shed some light on it. I need your help. I'm flying solo here, and I need a spiritual wingman.

Yesterday, I felt certain that my call for help would be answered. Now, that hope was gone. My spiritual wingman wasn't coming for me. I was on my own. I couldn't help feeling sorry for myself, and I wallowed in self-pity for the better part of a month. But as my grief subsided, a deeper understanding emerged. I realized that Wayne's passing was part of a larger plan. Just as it was Wayne's destiny to write in his last blog post, "The last suit you wear doesn't need pockets," it was my destiny to reach out to him on the very day he could no longer extend a helping hand.

"There are no accidents in this universe."

This was one of Wayne's favorite sayings. He believed that everything happens for a reason, and that life's most important lessons are learned from its tragedies, not its triumphs. The lesson I'd learned from Wayne's passing was that I was not meant to connect with him physically. I was meant to reach out to him spiritually.

Which is exactly what I did.

And that's when he reappeared in my life.

OUR FIRST VISIT

IT STARTED OUT as a typical morning. I woke up around 3:00 a.m., same as always. Except it wasn't an idea I awoke to, it was Wayne. He stood beside my desk, gazing out my bedroom window. The silver light of an enormous full moon streamed in around him.

I sat up against the headboard and looked at him. Describing him is difficult. He was not a physical being, though physically he looked the same as when I saw him last. I can't call him an apparition either. He was a force, a presence, an aura, as if the sheer power of his spirit had left a physical impression on the world, like a wake produced by a massive ship. What struck me most about him was that, when I compared myself to him, I felt like I was the one lacking something. Perhaps true substance isn't measured by the mass we occupy but by the light we shine. If so, he was the most substantial figure I had ever seen.

My apartment was on the ninth floor of a Denver high-rise. The exterior wall of my bedroom was a floor-to-ceiling glass bay that spanned the full width of the room. At the center of that bay stood my desk. The view from there was spectacular: the Denver skyline in the foreground, framed from behind by the front range of the Rocky Mountains. At this hour, the downtown skyscrapers showed as black spires against the moonlit sky. The mountains showed as a jagged shadow running low across the horizon.

Wayne seemed enthralled by the view. He made a long, slow sweep of the horizon, as though tracing some invisible thread that connected it all: the moon, the mountains, the city and the sky. Then, as if satisfied that everything was still together, he turned to me and smiled.

"Hi John, I've been waiting for you."

I stared at him a long time, unable to speak. Emotions from his passing returned. The heartbreak. The sorrow. The regret. So many regrets! I should have called him more. I should have written him more. I should have told him just once how much he meant to me. I considered spilling my guts right then, but something about Wayne's expression told me no. He didn't look like a man who wanted to talk about past regrets. To be honest, he looked like a kid who had discovered a secret door at the back of his bedroom closet and wanted someone to explore it with him.

"I've come to an important realization," he announced cheerily. "Our participation in death is voluntary, and I've decided not to play a part in mine any longer. I'm returning to the role I've played all my life. Inspirational teacher."

I smiled at that. It was just like Wayne to sneak out on death like a school kid ducking out of after-school detention. It felt good to see his old enthusiasm. And his old defiance.

In death, as in life, the old *Scurvy Elephant** was refusing to play by the rules.

We talked about family first. I asked him if he was still in contact with them, and he nodded. "Sometimes I speak to them in whispers," he said. "Sometimes in ocean waves. But I can still get my message across to anyone who cares to listen."

That drew another smile from me. Then he asked me how I was doing, and my smile fell away. I told him I was doing okay, but he saw through my disguise. I could never hide my true feelings from him. This, I suppose, is one of the reasons I liked being around him so much, because I didn't feel the need to.

"I've felt your presence often over the last ten months," he said warmly. "I've sensed your moments of awe and inspiration, and your moments of doubt and pain. I went through the same highs and lows myself when my life's calling came calling for me. I wanted to reach out to you earlier, but you weren't ready. Like Buddhists say, *The lesson can't begin until the student shows up at the classroom.* I knew you'd come to me when the time was right."

I told him I was going to call him on my birthday, but my voice choked.

"If you think my passing came as a shock to you," he said, grinning, "you should have been in my slippers that night."

---

* As a child, Wayne returned from school one day, upset because his teacher called him a "scurvy elephant." When he shared this with his foster mother, she called the teacher who said, "Oh, that Wayne—he's always getting things wrong. I didn't call him a scurvy elephant. I said he was a disturbing element."

I couldn't help but laugh at that. Obviously, his passing hadn't taken away his sense of humor. It was a sad thought all the same. I reconsidered his question. *How was I doing?* The only answer I could come up with was this:

I feel half lost and half found.

Wayne nodded gently. "You're like a caterpillar that doesn't yet know it can fly. You've caught glimpses of your higher self. You see it like a strip of light shining underneath a closed door. Whether you know it or not, you are on a sacred quest to open that door and step into the light."

I liked his analogy of a caterpillar turning into a butterfly—half lost, half found. As for the "sacred quest" part, I wasn't so sure. I never considered what I was doing to be either sacred or a quest. I just wanted to feel the excitement of living again.

"That's what spirituality is all about," he said as if he knew what I was thinking. "It's not about finding God above you. It's about finding peace within you."

I loved this definition of spirituality. The less heavenly I imagined it, the more I was attracted to it.

"Deep down," he said, "everyone hungers for the same thing, to live a peaceful, purposeful, fulfilling life. The problem is that most people pursue that goal down the wrong path. They focus on amassing wealth, prestige, power, and acclaim. Alluring as these things are, the satisfaction they provide us is both temporary and incomplete. They leave us feeling empty in the very place we most want to feel full. Those who follow this path eventually find themselves surrounded by a collection of things that their soul doesn't want but their mind is afraid to lose. Rather than feeling contented, they just feel more stressed."

I'd never heard the word "stress" used in a spiritual context. For some reason, it felt appropriate to me.

"Most people have come to accept stress as normal," he said. "Life is stressful, they tell themselves as if they had uncovered a profound secret rather than surrendered to their shallowest fears. Stress is not a fact of life; stress is a psychological pollution that people produce when their internal energy is out of balance." Wayne turned toward the window and looked out at the night. "You can feel it anywhere people are gathered, a toxic cloud of collective anxiety that is invisible to the eye but choking to the soul. The stress gathers in the atmosphere like smog hanging over a polluted city, seeping into your perception like acid rain. It starts by eroding your sense of wonder and excitement. It ends by eroding your very health."

At that point, I grabbed my pen and notepad and started taking notes. Wayne saw me and smiled. Though I didn't realize it, our first class together had just begun.

As I wrote, Wayne paced the room. He walked in the space behind my desk, pivoting at one end of the room in front of a six-foot palm plant, and at the other end of the room in front of a file cabinet. Back and forth he went, like a swimmer taking laps of a pool. This is how he liked to lecture, always moving. Like the universe itself, he didn't like to stand still.

After half a dozen laps, he stopped next to my desk and turned to me. There was a gleam in his eye that suggested a whole new world was about to open up for me.

"Do you believe in the idea of a perfect meal?" he asked matter-of-factly.

A perfect meal?

"Yeah, a meal so perfect that it ends your hunger forever."

Of course not.

"It's an absurd idea. And yet a great many people hold that very belief about spirituality. They think that a perfect idea exists out there that, once discovered, will fulfill their soul forever." Wayne shook his head. "Spirituality isn't about finding the perfect idea, any more than nutrition is about finding the perfect meal. It's about finding the proper balance. Food fuels your body, love fuels your soul. Most people feed themselves too much of the former and not enough of the latter. They live in a state of psychological imbalance, bloated in their mind and body and starving in their soul."

That last line sounded familiar to me, so I asked him which book he wrote it in. Wayne looked at me and smiled. "The idea isn't mine," he said.

Who then? I asked.

"You," he said coolly then pointed at my box of notes under the desk. "It's in there, about halfway down the stack. By the way, your handwriting is atrocious, even worse than mine."

My eyes darted first toward the box, then back to Wayne, then back to the box. By the time my gaze settled back on Wayne, he was laughing.

"Do you remember writing it?"

No.

"I'll quote it for you then," he said, and then did just that, reciting the words as if they floated in the air in front of him. "The source of their imbalance is false identification, a fundamental misunderstanding of who they are and what they really need. They mistake a spiritual deficiency inside them for a material insufficiency around them. They think they need more things when what they really need is more love."

I sat in silence after that, with the stunned look of someone who had just felt the Earth shift underneath them. In a way, it had. Hearing Wayne quote something I had written affected me in a way that is hard to explain. I felt like the door that he had alluded to earlier—the one that stood between me and my divine light—had cracked open. Not enough to pass through yet, but enough to know it wasn't locked shut. That alone was amazing.

"Welcome to your sacred quest," he said through a grin.

I told him he sounded like a greeter at Walmart, and he laughed, then his expression stiffened. "You know more than you think, John. The notes you've gathered in that box may seem like random ideas, but they are anything but. Each idea represents a piece of a jigsaw puzzle. Individually, the pieces reveal very little, but together they add up to something remarkable. You've gathered the pieces. Now, it's time to assemble them."

Assemble them into what? I asked, my voice sounding more desperate than I had intended.

"An image of yourself that matches the full depth of your nature."

His answer surprised me. I felt certain he was going to say, '*Your soul*'.

"I did in a way," he said. "Your soul is one of the missing pieces of the puzzle, but it's not the only one. The image you have of yourself is full of holes."

In my mind, I saw an image of myself depicted on a jigsaw puzzle that was missing half its pieces. The image made me shudder.

"I like that analogy," he remarked. "But the holes I speak of aren't on the surface of your being, they are at your depth. You believe you have a soul, but you don't really know what it is. It haunts your dreams, but it's absent from your daily life."

I felt a chill as he said this. I pictured my soul as the ghost of my former self, the me who ventured joyfully through the days, and slept soundly through the nights. I'd lost touch with that version of me, buried him under a mountain of minutia that I'd amassed throughout my life. I could no longer reach my soul, but I could still hear its muffled cries, like a miner calling out from the bottom of a collapsed mine, "I'm alive. Come set me free."

I wrote a note. *Our soul knows how to reach us, but we don't know how to reach it.* I held it up for Wayne and he nodded.

"Everyone has an image of themselves that they live by," he said. "This image may be something specific like, '*I'm a child of God*', or it may be something vague like, '*I'm just me,*' but everyone pictures themselves as something."

I asked myself how I pictured myself. No answer came to mind.

"You're not alone," he lamented. "Most people give little thought to how they see themselves. This is a huge mistake. Your life is a reflection of your own self-image. See yourself shallowly and you will live shallowly. See yourself fully and you will live fully."

I considered his words. I assumed that by "seeing myself fully," he meant seeing myself as my soul.

Wayne shook his head. "Not as your soul," he said. "*From* your soul."

I didn't understand what he meant by this, but I liked the idea all the same. It had a certain feel to it: calm, peaceful, inviting. If this is what living from the soul felt like, I wanted to learn more about it.

Where do we start?

"By defining the problem."

Which is?

"Spiritual separation."

I recalled writing on that subject, something about how the surface of our psyche separates from the core of our psyche. I probed my mind for more details, but found nothing.

Wayne helped me out.

"Everyone is born fully connected with their soul," he said, quoting the composition I was trying to remember. "But over time, they separate from it. First, they lose touch with it, then they lose sight of it. A total eclipse of the soul."

I looked at him, awestruck. Obviously, he was more familiar with what I'd written than I was. I suggested that he assemble this jigsaw puzzle himself. You dictate, I told him. I'll transcribe.

He immediately waved me off.

"This is your vision John, not mine," he said. "I'll help you in any way I can, but the ideas you've gathered have chosen you to be their spokesman. You'll have to assemble the pieces yourself."

I was afraid he was going to say that. I glanced at my box of notes, its sides bulging like an overstuffed trash bag. There was no organization to what I'd written—no index, no table of contents, no bookmarks. This was like assembling a jigsaw puzzle whose pieces were hidden inside a haystack.

I looked back at Wayne. His expression was calm, radiant, serene. At that moment, he looked every inch the spiritual guru.

"What makes you think you'll have to search for the ideas you are looking for in there?" he asked. "They came to you on their own. They will assemble themselves on their own if you let them. Just get out of their way."

I wanted to believe him, so I did something totally out of character for me. I meditated. I closed my eyes and chanted, "Get out of the way. Get out of the way." I felt strange doing this, but I did it all the same.

After a few minutes, Wayne asked me if anything had materialized yet. I shook my head. No messages from the universe, just my own inner voice snidely remarking, *'I told you this New Age mumbo-jumbo was nothing but a load of…'*

Then it arrived, scrolling across my mind like stock quotes on a ticker tape. First, the title of the essay he'd quoted me from, *Soulmates with Ourselves*. Then the words themselves.

Holy crap! I said out loud as I opened my eyes. Across the room, Wayne was laughing. A moment later, I joined him. Nothing feels better than seeing your own inner skeptic rendered speechless by the force of a higher power.

"Spiritual logistics," he said. "The right idea delivered at the right time."

Words continued to scroll across my mind, and I jumped out of bed, my notes in hand. Moments later, I was writing at my desk. Wayne stayed with me a moment, watching me write. As he did, it occurred to me that we were working on this jigsaw puzzle as a team now, him providing the vision, me assembling the pieces. I thought back to the letter I wrote him on the night of his passing, specifically the part where I asked him to be my spiritual wingman. Wayne had never received that letter, but he had obviously gotten the message. And here he was answering the call. I was about to joke with him that he hadn't lost a nephew but gained a secretary, but I never got the chance. He whispered one last bit of encouragement, "Stay open to everything and attached to nothing" Then he left me to my work.

LESSON ONE

SPIRITUAL SEPARATION

The invisible animating entity that occupies the physical body. The sum total of the non-physical aspects of a human being.

—Greek definition of psyche.

"Problems are illusions in that they are concocted by our minds because we have come to believe that we are separate from our source."

—Dr. Wayne Dyer

"Use your soul or lose your soul."

—John Dyer

WE BEGIN BY defining the problem: spiritual separation. As we age, most of us lose touch with our soul. This separation creates a fracture in our psyche, a delamination of the surface of our inner being (our thoughts and physical sensations) from the core of our inner being (our spirit). We hollow ourselves out with our own shallow perceptions of ourselves. We see only the surface of ourselves, and so we maintain only the surface of ourselves. In doing so, we fall out of psychological balance. We become obsessed with the needs of our mind and body, and we forget about the needs of our soul.

Spiritual separation is a global phenomenon that affects millions of people across all lines of race, creed, and religion. Its symptoms are devastating: anxiety, addiction, hypertension, lethargy, and malaise. In the Western world, these afflictions are considered medical conditions and are treated with therapy and drugs. But their underlying cause is rarely diagnosed. Science only accepts phenomena that can be measured by physical instruments. Spirit is not quantifiable, so science dismisses it. The result is we treat the physical symptoms that can be measured rather than the spiritual source that cannot.

> *"So how can you tell if you are suffering from a spiritual disconnect? Ask yourself this key question: How do I feel most of the time? If your answer is that you feel anxious, anguished, hurt, depressed, or frustrated, then you have a spiritual disconnect."*
>
> —Dr. Wayne Dyer

If you feel this way, you are not alone. In today's culture, spiritual separation is hard to avoid. Our education, upbringing, and peer groups all contribute to creating a collective tide of rampant superficiality that gradually draws us away from our soul. We learn to judge everyone—including ourselves—not by what they are but by what they have. Wealth, power, knowledge, and status become the standards by which value is defined. Eventually, our obsession with possessions comes to dominate our lives. We become consumed with consuming, every waking moment engaged in a never-ending quest to expand our net worth of things.

In the midst of these shallow preoccupations, our neglected soul wilts like a sun-starved flower, giving rise to dysfunctions like stress, apathy, hopelessness, and despair. These problems are all different manifestations of the same spiritual hunger—our soul crying out for love. Love is the glue that holds us together. The moment we stop getting it, we start coming apart at the seams.

The good news is that the hollowing out of our psyche can be reversed. Our emaciated soul can be restored to health, and our psyche brought back into balance. We simply have to reconnect with our spirit.

> *"The problems of disease, disharmony, discord, fear, anxiety, scarcity, and displeasure are in our minds. When we have these problems, we find ourselves feeling alone, alienated, isolated, angry, hurt, and anguished. Yet when we truly reconnect to our source these feelings disappear."*
>
> —Dr. Wayne Dyer

Wayne was keenly aware of the connection between psychology and spirituality. And he was not alone. Carl Jung said, *"Every psychological problem is ultimately a matter of religion."* Abraham Maslow said, *"The spiritual life is part of the human essence. It is a defining characteristic of human nature, without which human nature is not fully human."* Even Sigmund Freud, an avowed atheist, acknowledged the power of spirit. *"Religion," he said, "is an illusion and it derives its strength from the fact that it falls in with our instinctual desires."*

Wayne saw spirituality as a natural extension of psychology, the soul of psychology, if you will. Spirituality wasn't merely for the religiously devout, it was for everyone because everyone is spiritual.

> *"Spirituality is very similar to health. Everyone has health. For some their health is excellent and for others it is poor, yet you cannot escape having it at some level or another. The same is true for spirituality. Every single human being is a spiritual being. We all have spirit."*
>
> —Dr. Wayne Dyer

We all sense that we have a soul. Our problem is, we aren't intimate with it. We don't know how to turn it on. We all want that intimacy. We crave it in every cell of our being. But try as we might to become soulmates with ourselves, we fail. We remain friends without benefits, acquaintances and nothing more.

And the reason for this, in my opinion, is because we don't know what our soul really is. Sure, most people see their soul as one thing or another. Some see it as a spiritual tracking device recording their behavior. Others see it as a membership in a private country club in the clouds. Still others see it as a revolving door of new lives.

These renditions of the soul all leave me wanting. They explain what the soul does in the afterlife, but they fail to adequately explain what it does in the here and now. As far as I'm concerned, a soul that we wait for is a soul that we waste. And that, in my opinion, is the problem with most religions. They're so focused on what happens in the next life, they fail to teach us how to live in this one.

Visions of the afterlife as an all-inclusive cosmic cruise may provide temporary comfort to your mind, but they will not ignite your spirit because they are not real. Look at it this way, if you believed in an imaginary stomach and you fed it imaginary food, would the hunger in your belly go away? No. This is how most people practice spirituality. They feed an imaginary soul imaginary spirituality. All the while, their real soul continues to starve.

Our true soul exists outside the boundaries of our physical form. Outside the lines of our rational understanding.

In a dimension all its own.

DAY TWO

I was having trouble with the word "dimensions" even as I wrote it. It felt like the right word to use. Still, it seemed a bit *New Age* for me. I was definitely not *New Age*. More like Old School. I needed help.

I was relieved then when I woke up the next morning to find Wayne pacing my bedroom. I sat up in bed and looked at him. Again, I was struck by his aura. He looked like a living portrait rendered by an impressionist painter. His physical presence had blurred, but his spiritual essence had sharpened.

There was a palpable excitement about him this morning. I could tell he had a lot on his mind.

I held him off long enough to grab a cup of coffee from the kitchen. When I sat down at my desk, Wayne jumped right into a conversation.

"Your theory that the soul exists in a separate dimension from the mind feels right to you, doesn't it?"

Yes, I said, sipping my coffee.

"Then follow it," he said encouragingly. "I've always been open to the possibility of dimensions of reality beyond the physical realm. And that's what you're saying, isn't it, that spirit exists within your physical form, and yet, at the same time, separate from your physical form?"

I nodded hesitantly. His summary was spot on, but again I was afraid the word "dimensions" might steer the conversation toward subjects like parallel universes, astral projection, and time travel.

"Woo-woo stuff," he said, grinning.

Yeah, I laughed. Woo-woo stuff.

"Dimensions aren't separate worlds you travel to," he explained. "They are separate fields of energy that don't directly interact with each other. Take light and sound, for example. When a light wave and a sound wave meet, they don't interact with each other. The two waves pass through each other as if the other doesn't exist. The same holds true for thought and spirit. Both waves exist within you, and yet they don't interact with each another. They are in the same space and yet a world apart."

I imagined two radio stations playing inside me, my thoughts broadcasting on one frequency, my spirit on another.

"That's a great way of looking at it," he said. "You've been taught to believe that your perception consists of your five physical senses and your brain. This view of perception isn't wrong, just incomplete. Your five physical senses, along with your brain, represent your shallow perceptual window. You have a deeper perceptual window as well, that of your soul. Your soul has no eyes, and yet it sees. Your soul has no nerves, and yet it feels. Your soul has no brain, and yet it comprehends." He looked at me and raised his eyebrows. "You can see through your shallow perceptual window, or you can see through your deep perceptual window, but you can't see through both windows at the same time."

His explanation felt right to me, but I was having a hard time picturing it. I mean, how do you visualize something that lies outside the boundaries of your imagination?

"Examining your own perception can be difficult," he conceded. "Like trying to use a microscope to examine itself. But it's essential that you do so. Those who don't understand their perception can't control their perception."

I loved his last line and wrote it down word for word. When I finished, I told him that I didn't have to give him credit for it since he no longer legally existed. You can't plagiarize a ghost.

Wayne laughed and kept walking.

"These windows view the same world," he said, "but they do so in very different ways. Through your shallow perceptual window, you see the world as separate forms of matter. Through your deep perceptual window, you see the world as interconnected flows of energy. Two different perceptual vantage points seeing two different versions of reality. Einstein called this phenomenon, *"Two contradictory pictures of reality."* I call it the paradox of perception, and for me, it comes down to this key question: Are you a body that has a soul, or a soul that has a body?

Which perspective is correct?

"Both are," he answered. "From your shallow perspective, you are a separate physical form: a body that has a soul. From your deep perspective, you are a connected flow of energy: a soul that has a body."

So, it doesn't matter which perspective I choose?

"I didn't say that," he responded without hesitation. "The difference is enormous and can be summed up with this analogy. Imagine a tree trying to determine whether it is the leaves of its being or the roots of its being. Both perspectives are accurate, so neither conclusion is wrong. But that doesn't mean the two perspectives are equal. The difference arises when the leaves on the tree begin to fall. If the tree sees itself as its roots, this circumstance is seen as no big deal. But if the tree sees itself as its leaves, it's a cause for panic."

Peace versus panic.

Wayne nodded. "Now you see the real benefit of reconnecting with your soul, not to book a ticket to the afterlife, but to experience inner peace in this life. Every living thing shares the same spiritual root system. Don't believe in this root system, and you separate yourself from it. At that point, you are living as the leaves of your being, and every gust of wind will make you tremble."

Gooseflesh broke out along my arms as he said this. Wayne called this sensation 'the tinglies' and he likened it to a warm shower running through him. To me, it felt like every cell in my body had stood up and shouted "Amen" together.

I wrote notes for several minutes. When I was done, I had a question.

How do I reconnect with my soul?

"Through a shift in your consciousness," Wayne answered flatly.

Consciousness. That was another troubling word for me. I'd heard it used so many times, and in so many ways, I'm not sure what it meant.

"You're having difficulty understanding consciousness because you are confusing consciousness with awareness. They aren't the same thing. Consciousness isn't a form of awareness. Consciousness is the chooser of your awareness."

The chooser of my awareness. An intriguing concept, but not easy to picture.

Wayne rubbed his chin for a moment, then let out a breath. "Go back to the idea of multiple perceptual windows inside you. Picture these windows stacked vertically in your psyche, like floors in a multi-story building. Your consciousness cycles between these perceptual floors like an elevator traveling between floors. When the doors of your perception open on a particular level, you see the world from that point of view."

An elevator. Of course! I flipped open a new page and wrote a title in the top margin. *Our Three-Dimensional Perception.* Then I set the pen at the top of the page and watched it dance.

LESSON TWO

OUR THREE-DIMENSIONAL PERCEPTION

"You are not your mind. You are not your body."

—Dr. Wayne Dyer

"Which are you? Matter or essence? Physical or metaphysical? Form or spirit? The answer is both, even though they appear to be opposites."

—Dr. Wayne Dyer

"Your mind is a great manager but a horrible CEO."

—John Dyer

MOST OF US assume that our perception is made up of our five physical senses and our brain, meaning we sense the world through sight, sound, scent, taste, and feel, and we interpret those sensations with our mind. This view of human perception, though technically accurate, is woefully inadequate in my opinion. Human perception is far more complex than that. And far more miraculous. Human beings possess three distinct perceptual dimensions: sensual, rational, and spiritual. Each dimension is endowed with both awareness and understanding. Each evolved at different times for different purposes. Each constitutes a layer in the overall framework of our three-dimensional perception.

To better understand this concept, let's start by examining the state of dreaming. When we dream, we generally aren't aware of the experience. We aren't *having* the dream as much as we *are* the dream. This is a one-dimensional experience—awareness without consciousness—and it is how most of us dream. But this is not how we experience conscious reality. When we are awake, we play a dual role in our perception. There is a part of us that perceives reality and another part of us that receives these perceptions.

To illustrate this, consider the phrase, *'I am thinking.'* Notice how it refers to two distinct entities, one having the thought and the other receiving it. Here are more examples. *'Why can't I stop thinking about that person?' 'Why am I always putting myself down?' 'Why can't I get that song out of my head?'* These statements all assume that we are separate from our thoughts.

We see this same separation when we refer to our bodies. Examples include, *'My knee is sore.' 'My stomach is grumbling.' 'I am dying of thirst.'* We assume that we are separate from our body.

The same is true when we refer to our spirit. *'You touch my soul.' 'You lift my spirit.' 'You are my soulmate.'* Again, we assume that our soul is separate from us.

As these examples demonstrate, we instinctively refer to our perception as multi-dimensional. Our instinct is correct in this regard, for this is precisely how human cognition is structured. Three perceptual dimensions—body, mind, and spirit—linked together by a separate entity, which we call consciousness.

Physical sensation: The body. This is our sensual awareness. It includes bodily sensations such as hunger, physical pleasure and pain, and sexual desire.

Thought: The mind. This is our rational awareness. It includes mental sensations such as reasoning, calculation, comparison, analysis, expectation, judgment, and imagination.

Spirit: The soul. This is our radiant awareness. It includes collectively manifested sensations such as intuition, inspiration, peace, purpose, abundance, serenity, and love.

Consciousness: The chooser of our awareness. Our consciousness serves as a bridge between these three perceptual levels, cycling between them like an elevator traveling between floors. As the doors of our consciousness open on the various perceptual levels, we perceive the world from that perspective.

To understand how our three-dimensional perception evolved, let's go back to when life first appeared on Earth.

A BRIEF HISTORY OF PERCEPTION

"Look deep into nature, and then you will understand everything better."

—Albert Einstein

Life began 3.5 billion years ago as single-celled organisms like bacteria and algae fighting for survival in Earth's primordial soup. Simple as these organisms were, they were aware. It was a rudimentary awareness to be sure, nothing more than the ability to sense light, water temperature, and food sources. But these organisms were aware of their surroundings, and of each other.

This was life at its simplest, but it wouldn't remain that simple for long. Perpetual growth is the mandate of the universe, and these single-celled organisms were heeding that call. They grew through collaboration, gathering into colonies that worked together toward the shared purpose of survival. Though these cells lacked the physical senses we currently associate with communication—sight, sound, and hearing—these cells were not only communicating with each other, they were coordinating their behavior, distributing workloads, and specializing their talents.

These cell colonies were intelligent. This despite the fact that not a single brain existed among them. In fact, the first brain wouldn't appear on Earth for several *billion* years. And yet these cell colonies were exhibiting all the characteristics of intelligence: comprehension, planning, and reasoning.

Over the eons, these cell colonies continued to expand. Cells emerged into tissues. Tissues emerged into organs.

Organs emerged into bodily systems. Each of these miraculous developments was accomplished without the benefit of a centralized brain. Ironically, even the brain itself is not the product of a brain, but a colony of brainless cells.

Seen in this context, the brain can be regarded as an accessory of evolution rather than its primary objective. It appeared rather late in the evolutionary game to address a specific problem: the sheer size of life's ever-expanding cell colonies. At some point, these colonies grew too large to effectively self-manage. There were too many internal functions to coordinate and too many external sensations to process. The result was cognitive overload. To survive, these colonies needed a way to process this onslaught of information.

Life needed an internal processor.

Life needed a brain.

With the emergence of a brain, life continued to evolve. Animals emerged: fish, amphibians, reptiles, birds, and mammals. In birds and mammals, consciousness emerged. And, in a few species, self-consciousness. Today, our three-dimensional perception represents the culmination of three billion years of perceptual evolution. Three perceptual levels—spiritual, sensual, and rational—linked together by consciousness, which serves as a bridge between them.

THE ROLE OF CONSCIOUSNESS

Consciousness evolved as a solution to the problem of a single living being possessing multiple perceptual streams. Imagine sitting in a movie theatre where three movies were playing simultaneously on the same screen. The result would be cognitive overload. A similar overload would occur inside us if we were conscious of all our streams of perception at once. We would quickly go insane.

Our consciousness is not aware itself. Rather, it tunes in to one of our perceptual streams like an elevator opening its doors on different levels of a building. We aren't aware of these shifts in our perception because they take place seamlessly, like a well-edited movie. And it's precisely because these shifts are seamless that most of us aren't aware of either our multi-leveled perception or our ability to choose which perceptual level we wish to tune into. The result is the loss of that choice. Our consciousness is transformed into an elevator with no internal buttons.

We become a slave to our external conditions and past conditioning, a pawn to whatever, or whomever, is pushing our buttons the hardest.

BABY GATE

My first memory of my uncle is not a memory. It's a story he told me of a night he spent babysitting at our house when I was a toddler.

It's late summer 1966. Wayne is watching me, my brother, and my sister while my parents go out for dinner and a movie. My sister is four. My brother is two. I am one. Needless to say, Wayne has his hands full. This night will be good training for him. He and his wife are expecting their first child in less than a month.

According to Wayne, the incident, which I've affectionately dubbed 'Baby Gate,' happened like this. Everyone is gathered in the family room. My sister is coloring with crayons at the coffee table. My brother is stacking cardboard blocks into makeshift walls which he then crashes through like Superman. I am roaming about the room, clad in a diaper and a pair of all-white leather walking shoes, eagerly practicing my newly acquired skill of upright locomotion. At some point during the evening, I wander unnoticed out of the family room and into the hallway leading to the basement stairway. The stairway is guarded by a baby gate, one of those wood and mesh contraptions that wedge themselves inside doorways. Normally secured, the baby gate has somehow come unlatched this evening. When I discover the unguarded stairwell, I decide to explore the basement.

My attempt to negotiate the stairs is not successful.

Now, if anyone wonders why a toddler still learning to walk would attempt to descend a staircase doesn't remember being a toddler. You don't ask why you explore things, you do so because they are there. At eleven months, I was already an accomplished climber, having summited most of the household furniture. I was also an experienced caver, having spelunked my way through all the lower-level kitchen cabinets. The basement no doubt seemed like the next item to be checked off on my baby bucket list.

How I actually descended the stairs remains a mystery. Theories include a front roll, a sideways spin, or a toboggan run down on my diaper-padded bottom. I like to imagine myself stepping boldly off the top landing, reciting Shakespeare: "*Once more unto the breach. The coward dies a thousand deaths, the valiant but once.*" We'll never know for sure. All Wayne could tell me for certain is that when he found me at the bottom of the stairwell, I wasn't crying, and I had taken off my shoes.

I was nineteen when Wayne told me this story. Afterward, we shared a good laugh. I asked him if he felt guilty about the incident, and he said yes at first, then he added, "On second thought, no. I was just trying to teach you to be a no-limit toddler."

DAY THREE

The next morning, I sat at my desk, reviewing the last section. The process was half editing the prose, half reviewing the content. I was writing and learning at the same time. Wayne arrived midway through the process, as the first glow of sunrise appeared on the horizon. He paced the room as I worked, sometimes stopping to gaze out the window, other times to look over my shoulder.

The basics, as I saw it, were this. We have three independent levels of perception—sensual, rational, and spiritual—which are tied together by consciousness like an elevator traveling between floors. Our failure to control our consciousness relegates us to a state of cognitive submission. We become pawns to our external circumstances and past conditioning.

"Congratulations," Wayne said from behind me. "You've made great progress. You should be proud."

I grinned like a school kid who'd just received an "A" on a term paper. Where's my gold star? I asked him.

"Where's my apple?" he replied and then began to pace.

I gathered the edited pages and laid them face down in a metal tray on my desk marked 'Manuscript.' Then I opened my notepad, ready for today's class.

Wayne walked to the end of the window bay where the palm plant stood. He examined the plant for a moment then shot me a look. "You know you're supposed to dust these things," he commented dryly.

I'm in-between housekeepers at the moment, I replied, matching his tone.

Wayne smiled as he ran his fingers over the fronds. The dust seemed to disappear under his touch. "You've successfully separated thought from spirit. That's a great start. Now I want you to focus on the key difference between them."

Which is?

Transcendence.

Transcendence. That was another troubling word for me. You came across it often in spiritual literature. It seemed that every soul-seeker wanted to transcend something. For most, it was their physical body, which made sense if you were sick, elderly, or infirm. I mean, who wouldn't want to escape a ship that was sinking? As for me, my body was a source of great pleasure. I didn't want to escape it. What I wanted to escape was my stress.

"Picture the ocean during a storm," Wayne said, still caressing the plant. "The surface is turbulent, but the depth remains calm. The same theory holds true for you. Your anxiety exists at the surface of your being. It does not exist at your depth."

This idea went back to seeing ourselves as the roots of our being rather than the leaves of our being. Peace versus panic.

"Yes," he said. "Trouble is, you don't know which parts of you constitute your surface, and which parts constitute your depth. Go back to your theory of body, mind, and spirit. How would you classify each of them, superficial or deep?"

I thought for a moment. Body was obviously superficial. Spirit was obviously deep. As for mind? I suppose that depended on what I was thinking about.

"So you're saying that shallow thoughts are shallow and deep thoughts are deep?" he asked.

Yeah, something like that.

Wayne shook his head. "This is a major stumbling block, John, one which has tripped up many soul seekers, including myself. You're searching for the core of your being by means of deep thinking. That can't be done. All your thoughts, regardless of their content, transmit along the surface of your psyche. Therefore, all your thoughts, at least perceptually speaking, are shallow."

It was strange to hear Wayne say this. He'd spent his life preaching the power of positive thinking.

"That hasn't changed," he insisted. "I've always believed in thinking positively. I've simply evolved my definition of what a positive thought is. Not a thought with a happy message per se, but a thought that is aligned with the deeper awareness of spirit."

That made sense. Sort of.

"I'll give you an example," he said. "Consider the thought, *I am strong*. On its face, it seems positive, but it really depends on how you use it. If you tell yourself, *I am strong* in response to a disparaging comment made toward you, then the thought is an expression of strength and, therefore, positive. But if you tell yourself, *I am strong* in order to feel superior to someone else, then the thought is an expression of weakness and therefore negative. Same thought, opposite effect. It all depends on the intention—the spirit—behind the thought."

I liked the idea of judging my thoughts by their alignment with my underlying spirit. That made sense, like judging the health of a tree by the condition of its roots rather than the condition of its leaves. But I was still unclear as to what I was aligning my thoughts with. What was this deeper level of awareness we call spirit?

Wayne nodded knowingly, as if anticipating this question. He turned toward the window and looked up at the sky.

"All my life," he said, "I've strived to raise my consciousness by discovering higher levels of awareness. During the first half of my life, I focused on elevating my thoughts. This strategy proved successful, but over time I realized that my journey was not complete. I began catching glimpses of another level of awareness inside me, one which transmits on a frequency so high it transcends our physical form entirely. This awareness, which we call spirit, is not part of us, we are part of it. One shared energy that is created by all and flows through all. One shared root connecting everything that has no beginning or end."

Wayne turned back toward me and spread out his arms, as though presenting himself as a visual aid. "I stand here before you, fully detached from thought, and yet fully present in spirit, and I can tell you without reservation that thoughts are a bodily function."

But wait, I argued. Thoughts are energy, formless, massless, shapeless. They can't be part of our body.

"That's a trick your mind is playing on you," Wayne countered. "Don't fall for it. Your heartbeat and your metabolism are fields of energy, and you consider them to be part of your body."

Good point.

"In fact, you consider all your bodily functions to be part of your physical form, except one: your thoughts."

I tried comparing my thoughts to my perspiration. My mind didn't like the comparison at all.

"Don't let your mind fool you into thinking it's special. It's not. Everything that is contained within your physical form is part of your physical form, regardless of whether it's matter or energy. This includes your heart and your heartbeat. It also includes your mind and your thoughts. You don't identify yourself with your heartbeat or your metabolism, do you? So why would you identify yourself with your thoughts?"

Again, a good point.

"Your mind has convinced you that it is the core of your being when it is really just part of your outer shell. This misguided belief has created a false bottom to your identity, a fake floor of deep thoughts that you mistakenly believe are your spirit. These spiritual thoughts may resemble spirit, but they lack the power of spirit. They can't provide you with the deep emotional nourishment you need to be fulfilled."

So I have to stop thinking?

"No," he said adamantly. "You have to stop identifying yourself with your thoughts. Thoughts are important, and you should make a concerted effort to cultivate them, but always with the understanding that they are a tool of your spirit, not a substitute for your spirit. Use your thoughts like any other part of your body, just don't attach yourself to them. When you do, your thoughts transform from instruments of your spirit to shackles on your spirit."

I searched inside myself for a level of awareness beyond my thoughts. I found nothing.

"Of course, you found nothing," he remarked gently. "You're using your mind to search for spirit. That's like using a radio to try to detect light. Your soul is not something you can see, hear, smell, or taste. You don't find it by searching for it. You find it by turning it on."

That idea sent a surge of tinglies through me. More would follow.

"That which is most substantial about you has no substance at all," he said. "Your soul is both the core of your being and, at the same time, not contained within your being. It's in the flesh, but not of the flesh."

In the flesh, but not of the flesh. Another intriguing concept, but again not easy to visualize.

"Picture a sea sponge floating in the ocean," Wayne explained. "The water flowing through the sponge is an integral part of its being. The sponge can't survive without it. And yet that same life-sustaining water isn't contained within the sponge. It's in the sponge, but not of the sponge. Spirit is to you what water is to a sea sponge. In you, but not of you. Invisible, yet essential. Without it, you're an empty shell."

I wrote a note: *In form, we are rocks, but in spirit, we are sponges.* Then I reviewed what we had discussed this morning.

Physical vs. Metaphysical. The physical aspects of our nature include both our material form and the energy that is contained within that form. Thoughts, respiration, and digestion are all fields of energy that are contained within our physical form. This makes them physical. Spirit is a field of energy that transcends our physical form. This makes it metaphysical.

Transcendence. Not leaving our physical form, but freeing ourselves from our psychological attachment to our physical form. To complete ourselves, we must connect with a power outside ourselves. We can only do this on one level of our being: Our spirit.

The Soul. Not an organ within us but an awareness passing through us. One shared psychological energy that runs through the fabric of all living things.

Enlightenment. Not discovering our soul but igniting our soul. Seeing the world through the cleansing light of love.

I looked up for my spiritual wingman, but he was gone. I flipped open a new page and continued writing.

LESSON THREE

OUR TRANSCENDENT SPIRIT

"Spirit is a dimension beyond beginnings and ends, beyond boundaries, beyond symbols, and beyond form itself."

—Dr. Wayne Dyer

"There is another dimension that is very much a part of you, which has nothing to do with logic or scientific validation."

—Dr. Wayne Dyer

"The song the soul sings is never a solo."

—John Dyer

LET'S START WITH a simple question, which one of the trillions of cells that make up your body is 'you?'

The answer, of course, is none of them. You aren't any one of your constituent cells. You are the life force that extends through them all. With that in mind, ask yourself this question. If the life force that is *You* extends beyond the boundaries of any one of your constituent cells, couldn't it also extend beyond the boundaries of them all?

The answer, paradoxically, is both yes and no. Your thoughts and physical sensations are confined within your physical form while your spirit transcends your physical form. This is why no one can read your thoughts, but everyone can sense your spirit. Spiritual energy flows through all living things, like water flowing through a sea sponge.

Now, the idea of transcendence may sound incredible to you, but it's really quite ordinary. Picture a sound wave and a light wave as they come into contact with a pane of glass. The sound wave reflects off the glass while the light wave passes through the glass. No one considers it miraculous that light flows through glass, it's simply an attribute of light. Light penetrates glass, sound does not. It's not a miracle, it's physics.

The same theory holds true for thought and spirit. Our thoughts are contained within our physical form while our spirit passes through our physical form. This isn't a miracle, it's physics.

Examples of spirit are everywhere. It's the electricity in the air of a sports arena, and the rush of a city that never sleeps. It's the vibe in a concert hall as the house lights go down, and the tension in a courtroom as the verdict is about to be announced. It's the serenity of a church, and the tranquility of nature. The thrill of the Vegas strip, and the calm of a country lane. The butterflies dancing in your stomach, and the chills creeping across your skin. It's cleansing tears of laughter and crushing tears of sorrow. In short, spirit is everything we feel together, the palpable yet indescribable energy that radiates through all living things.

What triggers spirit? Could be anything: a thought, an action, a touch, a song, a beautiful vista. Anything that ignites the soul. Since all living things radiate spiritual energy, spirit isn't limited to human beings. A redwood tree is made up of trillions of living cells, all radiating a song that the soul can hear. Primal energy being broadcast by life's primal source.

We all long to feel spiritual energy, which is why we attend gatherings like church services, concerts, movies, lectures, and sporting events. Though we can experience these events remotely via television or the internet, we feel drawn to experience them with other people.

Why?

Because we all want to feel spirit's power.

Spirit not only flows through living things, it can build between living things. Ideas, songs, prayers, and movies all radiate energy. This energy is amplified when we share these experiences with others whose intentions are aligned with ours. This is why singing alone in the shower is not as satisfying as singing with others at a concert. There is an energy generated by the crowd that moves us in a way we just can't feel on our own. And what moment of a concert moves us the most? When the singer holds the microphone out to the crowd and says, "Sing it with me."

And everyone does.

This is the power of spirit, and we are drawn to it like plants to the sun. Spirit excites us and calms us, energizes us and grounds us, elevates us and unites us, empowers us, and humbles us. It's the feeling of being aligned on all our levels, our inner symphony playing in tune.

Can living things really share spiritual energy? Of course. Your own physical form is living proof. Every cell in your body is a separate living thing. These cells are not components of you. You are a collaboration of them. Cells collaborate to form tissues, tissues collaborate to form organs, organs collaborate to form bodily systems, bodily systems collaborate to form human beings. Human beings can likewise collaborate with others. The miracle of divine collaboration has no end. There is literally no limit to how miraculous we can become. On the physical plane, we have set boundaries, but on the spiritual plane, the sky is the limit.

Now, you may ask yourself, 'If spiritual energy is so powerful, why don't I feel it?' The answer is simple. Because you're blocking it out with your own shallow perception of yourself. Psychologically speaking, your self-image is self-fulfilling. Whatever you see as your psychological boundaries become those boundaries. If you see yourself as confined to your physical form, you *are* confined to that form. A psychological wall goes up around you that prevents you from sharing spiritual energy. But if you see through your psychological boundaries, you dissolve those boundaries. You can project yourself into the living things around you and, in doing so, combine spiritual energy with them.

That said, I agree that the current state of humanity's collective spirit is poor. But this isn't because the power of spirit is weak, it's because we, masquerading as individuals, have made it weak. We must be in sync with our spirit or there is no real spirit at all, just countless individual frequencies all canceling each other out. The sweeping tide of spiritual emptiness that most of us languish in every day.

The truth is, we are all transcendent beings, spirits who can soar beyond the boundaries of ourselves. Most of us have simply "un-transcended" ourselves by limiting our perception to our five physical senses and our mind. Spirit is not our sixth sense. Spirit is our first and highest sense. And yet, because our physical senses can't perceive spirit, and our mind can't understand spirit, most of us dismiss spirit altogether, deeming it an illusion or an anomaly rather than the essence of who we are. Our thoughts are the real anomalies of our nature, the ghosts in the larger machine of life's collective spirit. The soul can't be seen, nor can it be rationally understood. It's the sight beyond our eyes, the understanding beyond our rationale. We can't see our soul. We can only see from it.

LEARNING TO SWIM

It's a February morning in 1971. My brother and I are at the indoor swimming pool of Mercy High School in Farmington, Michigan, where my uncle works as a guidance counselor. Wayne is with us, along with his daughter Tracy, my cousin. Tracy is four and already swimming like a fish. I am five, and my brother is six. Neither of us can swim.

Still, like all children, we love the water and are having a ball playing on the steps leading into the shallow end of the pool. We hang from the handrail like monkeys, squirt water at each other through clenched palms, propel ourselves across the steps like human torpedoes. It's winter in Michigan, and we are in a pool. We couldn't be happier.

I don't realize anything is wrong until I'm drying off on the pool deck and I see my brother run past me, closely pursued by two lifeguards. I'm immediately confused. Why are the lifeguards chasing him? What has my brother done wrong?

Unbeknownst to me or my brother, we are here to learn to swim. We will do so under the tutelage of Mercy High School's Phys-Ed teacher, a stout middle-aged German woman named Mrs. Grimm. Mrs. Grimm has an unorthodox approach to teaching children to swim. Buddhists have a saying, "*One must learn how to die before they can learn how to live.*" Mrs. Grimm held a similar conviction when it came to teaching swimming. *One must learn how to drown before they can learn how to swim.* Specifically, this meant that your first swim lesson didn't involve actual instruction. Rather, it consisted of you being thrown off the diving board into the deep end to assess your natural aptitude.

Seriously.

I call this the waterboarding method of swim instruction, and it goes like this. Two lifeguards "escort" you to the end of the diving board and tell you to jump. Failure to comply with their directive leads to enhanced incentive techniques, including nudging, shoving, or outright tossing—whatever it takes. You depart from the diving board and are plunged into twelve feet of water, where you flail about for half a minute while Mrs. Grimm examines your technique. Eventually, she swoops in to save you. She hauls you to the surface, tows you to the side of the pool, and plops you on the deck. As you gasp for air, she tells you what you did wrong.

Seriously.

My brother would be today's first victim, and like many kids, when the lifeguards tell him to walk out onto the diving board, he instead runs for his life. My brother is fast, and he manages to elude his pursuers for several laps around the pool, but once the lifeguards split up, his fate is sealed. The lifeguards grab him by the arms, haul him back to the diving board, and walk him out to the end like a condemned pirate. At the edge, they tell him to jump. My brother stands there for a trembling moment, then the lifeguards shove him in. He splashes into the water and disappears for what seems like many minutes to me. Finally, Mrs. Grimm surfaces with him. She is already telling him what he did wrong.

"No good," she bellows. "You don't walk in water, you swim." Useful information for those who know how to swim. Not so useful to those who don't. Mrs. Grimm tows my brother to the side of the pool and plops him on the deck. He is coughing, gagging, and crying. As far as I can tell, he is no closer to being able to swim.

Witnessing this from the other side of the pool, I experience two emotion: sympathy for my brother, and relief for myself. That I will be spared this torture, I have no doubt. The Geneva Convention may have sanctioned waterboarding on six-year-olds, but surely not on five-year-olds. I was in kindergarten, for pity's sake. Naps are part of the curriculum. Extra credit is coloring inside the lines. No one could be so heartless as to toss a kindergartner wearing a Captain America bathing suit into the deep end of a pool.

Mrs. Grimm extends a bony finger toward me.

Time slows to a crawl, and I watch in muted horror as the lifeguards approach. They pick me up like a duffel bag, carry me to the end of the diving board, and hold me out over the edge. I look down at the water. It looks deep, dark, and angry. Mrs. Grimm treads water to one side like a stalking shark.

I remember falling, the sound of the splash as I hit the water, bubbles all around me, then silence. How long she let me flounder under there, I don't remember, but I think she secretly enjoyed it. Eventually, she hauls me to the surface, tows me to the side of the pool, and deposits me next to my brother, where I join him in a chorus of blubbering.

This was my first exposure to alternative learning techniques. Many of these unconventional practices would prove effective. This one, not so much. My brother and I did eventually learn to swim. It happened the following summer, and it wasn't Mrs. Grimm who taught us. One lesson Mrs. Grimm did teach me was about learning, and about fear. Fear may be an effective learning device, but the price we pay for it is too high. What is learned in fear is tainted with fear. Amassing knowledge without love is like hoarding spoiled food. The more you feed on it, the sicker you become.

DAY FOUR

As I lay in bed that night, I thought about how often I used phrases that identified me with my thoughts. *'I'm thinking about changing my diet.' 'I think I'll go to the store.' 'Let me think about that for a moment.'* I tried comparing this to how often I used phrases that identified me with my spirit. And that's when it hit me. I couldn't think of a single word to describe the act of expressing our soul. A few words hinted at the idea: sensing, intuiting, and knowing. But they all seemed inadequate. Perhaps no suitable word existed for expressing our soul. If true, it would explain why we have such a hard time doing it. Everyone knows they have a soul, but no one knows how to use it.

* * *

The next day began much like the previous one. I was up before dawn, editing the last section. Wayne arrived just after sunrise and was now pacing the room. After half a dozen laps, I told him I was glad he was a ghost, because if he had actual feet, he would have worn a hole in my carpet by now. He laughed and kept walking, gathering material for today's class.

I had a better grasp of human perception now. We perceive the world in two directions at once (proactively and reactively), and in three dimensions at once (sensually, rationally, and spiritually). Whichever of these perceptual currents is most powerful at any given moment is what we are aware of in that moment.

For me, the most powerful perceptual current always seemed to be my thoughts. Over the last twenty-four hours, I had made multiple attempts to shift my awareness to my soul. None were successful. Seems I could conceptualize the idea of seeing from my soul, but I couldn't actually do it. Perhaps my consciousness was like an out-of-order elevator, its doors stuck open on the level of my mind.

"That's closer to the truth than you realize," Wayne remarked as he made another lap of the room. "Years of formal training in rational thinking has energized your mind to the point where it dominates your perception. You can't consider anything from any perspective other than rationally thinking about it. Occasionally, you experience moments of spirit: in nature, at a concert, or at a religious service. In these places, the spiritual energy is strong enough to penetrate your stream of thoughts. But in your daily life—at work, in a shopping mall, or stuck in a traffic jam—the spiritual energy doesn't have the power to penetrate your veil of thoughts. And so you aren't aware of spirit. Instead, you're aware that you are tired, or that it's raining, or that the person driving in front of you is going 15 mph below the posted speed limit."

Whatever pushes our buttons the hardest.

"Yes," Wayne said as he passed behind my desk. "But don't forget, perception is a two-way street. You *can* control it from the inside, but not until you learn to measure the energy behind each perceptual current."

So I have to audit my perceptual energy?

"Yes."

I pictured myself inventorying my psyche like a retail clerk taking stock of a store's back room. *'Ten cases of rational awareness...check. Four cases of sensual energy...check. Half a case of internal lightbulbs...time to order more.'*

My spiritual wingman suppressed a grin. "Let's start with sensual energy. Are you hungry right now?"

No.

"Are you in pain?"

No.

"Do you feel ecstatic, euphoric, or overjoyed?"

No.

"So your sensual energy is low. That would change quickly if the stapler on your desk fell on your big toe. Sensual energy, in the form of pain, would shift your attention to your sensual awareness. And there, your attention would remain until the pain subsided and another perceptual flow eclipsed it."

This made sense. Attention goes where energy flows. And vice versa. Perception is a two-way street.

"That's good," he said. "Now, let's move on to spirit. What's the energy level in your soul this morning?"

I looked at him blankly. How do I measure that?

"By the presence of two coexisting emotions: enthusiasm and serenity. You feel like anything is possible, and yet nothing needs to be done."

I examined my own emotional state. I felt exactly the opposite: apathetic and anxious, like nothing really mattered, but something always needed to be done.

Wayne gave me a sympathetic nod. "That's a sure sign that your thoughts have eclipsed your spirit. You're all noise and no light. Which brings us to your third level of awareness: your thoughts. What's the energy level in your head right now?"

I glanced at my coffee mug, my third cup. Despite all the caffeine, I felt sluggish.

Low as well, I told him.

"Don't be so sure," he shot back. "Sluggishness is not a sign of mental lethargy, it's a sign of mental frustration. Your brain is working overtime without achieving the result you really want. To feel good."

Then I guess I don't know how to measure my mental energy. How do I do it?

"Stop thinking for a minute," he answered flatly.

Stop thinking?

"Yeah. Turn your mind off for sixty seconds, then turn it back on."

I closed my eyes and took a deep breath, trying not to think. Honestly, I didn't expect to go a full sixty seconds without having a thought, but what really shocked me was how difficult it was to go five seconds without one. Literally, the moment I extinguished one thought, another one emerged. The disturbing idea occurred to me that not five seconds of my life had gone by without some color commentary from my brain.

"If you pay attention to your internal dialogue," Wayne said, "you will see that you aren't always in control of it.

Oftentimes, it's the thoughts themselves that are driving the conversation. Listen to the back and forth going on inside your head and you will see what I mean. Your mind is constantly telling you what to do. *'Go here.' 'Do this.' 'Slow down.' 'Speed up.' 'Remember this.' 'Don't forget that.'* If another person bossed you around like this, you would tell them to shove it. But you accept it from your own mind under the mistaken belief that its voice is really *You.*"

I pictured a navigation app running inside my head, constantly barking out directions.

"Yes," he said, his voice gaining force. "And that's only half the story. If your mind isn't telling you what you should be doing in the future, it's no doubt telling you what you should have done in the past. It does this everywhere. At home: *"You're late for work again. I guess the fifth time hitting the snooze button was one too many."* At work: *"You got passed up for another promotion. No surprise there. You've never been assertive enough."* Even in a grocery store check-out-line: *"Congratulations. You managed to pick the slowest lane again. It's your God-given gift."*

Wayne's last example made me chuckle. I'd muttered words to that effect on several occasions.

"People see their mind as a great problem solver," Wayne said. "And it is. But if you observe your thoughts during times when there are no real problems, you will see that your mind is mostly occupied with either analyzing the past or planning for the future."

Judgment and expectation.

"Yes," he said. "Judgment and expectation are the mind's busywork, the product of its never-ending compulsion to find a solution in every moment, whether a problem exists in it or not. This busy work is not only pointless, it is, by its very nature, negative. Your thoughts are currents of energy that flow through your brain. Left unchecked, these currents can strengthen to the point where they take control of your consciousness. Your attention is constantly diverted from the present moment to either an expectation of the future or a judgment of the past. In the midst of this mental vortex, you grow increasingly more detached, anxious, and negative."

Wayne's analogy of a mental vortex reminded me of summers in my childhood when my friends and I would create whirlpools in my neighbor's above-ground circular pool. We would spread out along the pool's perimeter, like spokes on a wheel, and walk in a large circle, everyone moving in the same direction. After a few laps, a current emerged, weak at first but steadily gaining force. Soon we were jogging to keep up with the current, then leaping. Eventually, the current swept us off our feet. It occurred to me that our thoughts operate much like the water in that pool. When they are calm, we control them. But when they grow too strong, they control us.

I made a note. *A manic mind creates a depressive life.* Afterward, I continued writing. Out of the corner of my eye, I saw Wayne smiling. Once again, he'd led me to the trailhead of a new idea and then set me off to explore it on my own.

LESSON FOUR

INVENTORYING OUR ENERGY

"Our inner worlds are a frenetic beehive of activity with the same thoughts endlessly repeating themselves."

—Dr. Wayne Dyer

"Those who chase their thoughts lose their soul."

—John Dyer

I START THIS section by asking a few questions:

- Do you feel fully connected with your life? Or do you feel detached from it somehow, like you are experiencing your life from behind a glass screen?
- Is your life comfortable, prosperous, secure, and yet still not fulfilling?
- Do you find yourself trending toward cynicism, pessimism, and irritability?

If you are experiencing these symptoms, you are not alone. Most people feel world-weary to some degree. We all remember a time, usually as young children, when life was new and exciting, a fresh revelation every day. We understood little about ourselves and even less about the world around us. And yet our lives were full of wonder and enchantment. We were excited, enthused, happy.

So what happened to us? Did we make a wrong turn somewhere, inadvertently sailing out of life's trade winds and into its doldrums? How did the wind fall out of our sails?

The truth is, we didn't make a wrong turn in our lives, we made a wrong shift inside ourselves. We learned to define, analyze, and judge everything we see. We like to call this process "comprehending" reality, but it might be better described as the warehousing of reality, packing the world into mental boxes and then stacking them on shelves inside our head. The more we practice this mental compartmentalization, the better we get at it. Eventually, the process becomes automated. The moment we see something, we've already filed it away in some mental compartment. We become living, breathing warehouses of information: organized, efficient, and lifeless.

To illustrate this, imagine a cool breeze blowing over you on a hot summer day. The breeze feels good on your skin, and you savor the sensation for a moment. Now, you could continue relishing the moment by remaining connected to your sensual awareness, but more than likely you won't. Your mind will butt in, offering an analysis of the situation that you neither asked for nor needed.

> *"That breeze feels wonderful, but a cold front in summer usually means a storm is coming, and*

> *I didn't bring an umbrella with me because the weatherman assured me there was no chance of rain today."*

Try the Buddha test sometime. Gaze at a flower and try to appreciate it without thinking. More than likely you can't.

> *"That flower sure is beautiful. A tulip, I think. Lucky to see one blooming this time of year. Tulips don't do well in the heat. Oh, why didn't I plant that vegetable garden I always talked about? Fresh vegetables on the table every day would be great. What time is it anyway? Oh God, it's 4 pm, and I haven't checked off a single item on my to-do list."*

These are two examples of how an over-amplified mind can push the CALL button on your consciousness, shifting your attention from your sensual or spiritual awareness to a stream of mental abstractions running through your head. It's like experiencing your life through a series of self-generated postcards. *Here I am looking at a flower. Here I am feeling a cool breeze. Here I am wondering if it's going to rain.* The more you engage in these mental abstractions, the more you energize them. At a certain level of power, they take control of your consciousness, creating a vortex of conditioned thought patterns that you are trapped within.

These conditioned thought patterns wouldn't be a problem if they were positive, but generally they are not. And this has nothing to do with the content of your thoughts but rather the energy level behind them. If the energy of your thoughts is stronger than the energy of your spirit, you tend to focus on the negative. If the energy of your spirit is stronger than the energy of your thoughts, you tend to focus on the positive.

To understand this phenomenon, we must examine the environment in which life evolved.

REMNANTS OF A HOSTILE WORLD

> *"In times of peace, prepare for war."*
>
> —Publius Flavius Vegetius Renatus

> *"At a certain level of energy, there is no such thing as a positive thought."*
>
> —John Dyer

Primordial Earth was a hostile place for living things. Mortal threats abounded: starvation, disease, exposure, drought, and floods. Add to this the constant threat of becoming a predator's next meal, and the inherent hostility of the world was glaringly apparent to all living things.

In the midst of this hostile environment, life adapted its internal programming. It became defensive. *Trust no one. Doubt everything. Never let your guard down.*

This was the stark reality for life on Earth for three billion years. But over the last few centuries, that situation changed, at least for human beings. Humanity has managed to overcome the greater bulk of Earth's mortal threats. This shift from a primarily hostile environment to a primarily friendly environment occurred very quickly by evolutionary standards, far too quickly for human beings to have adapted to yet. And so, though our environment has changed, our internal programming has remained the same.

Trust no one. Doubt everything. Never let your guard down.

The human mind, in a state of fear, is programmed to deal with hostility, not tranquility. Threats are what it looks for, and threats are what it finds. This remains true regardless of the situation. Present a fearful mind with the scenario of a tiger charging at you, and it responds with panic. Present a fearful mind with the scenario of a stranger approaching down a dark alley, and it responds with apprehension. Present a fearful mind with the scenario of a sunny day at the beach, and it responds by wondering if this month's mortgage payment went out on time.

In fact, a fearful mind is so good at ferreting out problems that it will find one even when presented with two positive options, like choosing between steak or lobster at a restaurant. Order the steak and you will wonder if the lobster was better. Order the lobster and you will wonder the same thing about the steak. Whatever you choose, your mind will find a problem with it.

Problems are the purpose of the mind. That's what the mind is designed to do: identify, prioritize, and solve problems. By its very nature, the mind doesn't know how to deal with a state of "no problem." If something is not a problem, an overenergized mind will continue to analyze it until it becomes a problem. This is how the mind works when it's not guided by a higher spiritual purpose. If it doesn't have real problems to solve, it will start manufacturing problems on its own.

These problems may be imaginary, but our emotional responses to them are not. Our bodies react to imaginary problems the same way they act to real problems: with fear. This fear amplifies our negative thought patterns, increasing their intensity and thus strengthening their presence inside our heads. Eventually, a vicious cycle emerges. The more we focus on our problems, the more prominent they become. The more prominent our problems become, the more we focus on them.

This cycle of fear and negativity is the very definition of psychological suffering, and it continues to plague humanity today. It's the worst kind of poverty there is, a scarcity of spiritual energy. The crushing poverty of the soul.

A LEAP OF FAITH

It's early summer, 1976, and Wayne pulls into our driveway in his Volkswagen wagon.

The car sits low in the back, weighed down by a dozen cases of Wayne's latest book stowed in the rear compartment. The book is called *Your Erroneous Zones*, and it speaks of how to free yourself of emotional turmoil by changing your habitual thinking patterns. It's Wayne's first book aimed at a non-academic audience.

Sales of *Your Erroneous Zones* have been strong in New York City, where Wayne has promoted it on local radio stations. He is convinced the book will appeal to a national audience if presented to it, but since his publisher has no plans to promote it, Wayne decides to do it himself. He buys every remaining copy, packs them into his car, and embarks on a self-financed cross-country book tour.

I smile as my uncle steps out of his car. There is an infectious energy about him, and within minutes a crowd of neighborhood kids gather around him. We toss a football in the yard, shoot baskets in the driveway, and show off our latest skateboard tricks on the street.

Just before dinner, my uncle David arrives, and the three brothers—Wayne, David, and Jim (my dad)—are reunited, an occasion they are well accustomed to, having been separated from each other for much of their youth. After dinner, my mom breaks out a photo album of the three brothers. Everyone comments on the resemblance between Wayne and me when we were toddlers.

Wayne spends the night on our couch and is off the next morning to continue his tour. He has two interviews in Detroit this morning and two more in Cleveland this afternoon. From there, he's on to Columbus, Cincinnati, Indianapolis, St. Louis, and all points west.

As Wayne pulls out of our driveway, I notice the apprehension on my parents' faces. He has left a tenured professorship at St. John's University, along with a thriving therapy practice, to sell books out of the back of his car.

I'm too young to understand their concern. All I see is my uncle driving down the street, his head sticking out the window like a dog with its nose in the wind. There isn't a shred of fear in him. Something about that look draws me in. It's the way I want to travel, the way I want to live.

Like a dog with its nose in the wind.

DAY FIVE

When Wayne arrived the next morning, I wasn't in the bedroom to greet him. I was in the kitchen fetching another cup of coffee after editing the last section. When I returned to the bedroom, I saw him standing beside my desk, staring at the edited pages. His expression was solemn, brooding, deliberate. It reminded me of how my father looked when he reviewed one of my high school report cards.

All morning, I'd been worried about how Wayne would react to the last section. One line in particular concerned me: "*At a certain level of energy, there is no such thing as a positive thought.*" How would the father of positive thinking respond to that?

Wayne didn't make eye contact with me as I approached. Another bad sign. I sat at my desk and sipped my coffee in silence. After several minutes, he turned to me. To my surprise, he was smiling.

"I like how you've defined positive thinking," he said, "Not by the content of your thoughts, but by their energy in relation to your underlying spirit. As long as the light of your spirit shines through the veil of your thoughts, your thoughts remain positive. But the moment either your spirit grows too dim, or your veil of thoughts grows too thick, your soul is eclipsed, and your thoughts go dark." He tapped his fingers on the desk and nodded. "I like it. I like it a lot."

Thanks, I said. Where do we go next?

"You've inventoried your energy. That's an important step. Now comes the hard part."

Which is?

"Inventorying your fear"

My fear? I smirked at him. What's there to inventory?

Wayne raised his eyebrows. "That's your fear expressing itself right there, John. Denial is a form of fear, perhaps the worst kind of it—fear that you don't know you have. The truth is, you've spent most of your life in fear."

A shiver ran through me as he said this, as if his words had opened a secret door inside me. I wiped away my smirk and paid attention.

"How do you picture fear?" he asked.

Two images came to mind. First, someone running from a wild animal. Second, someone trembling in a corner.

"Terror and paralysis. That's how most people picture fear. But the spectrum of fear encompasses far more than that. Greed is fear—fear of not having more. Ambition is fear—fear of not accomplishing more. Envy is fear—fear of not being more. Anger, indifference, resignation, cynicism, lust, avarice, and pride—all are forms of fear."

I thought about what he said. I had never considered ambition, indifference, anger, and pride to be expressions of fear. If true, then what he said was accurate, a large portion of my life was spent in fear.

"Taking stock of your fear is the next step on your journey," he said, "And I warn you, it won't be easy. The foe you face is more formidable than you can imagine, an invisible force hidden inside you that is constantly changing forms, shifting seamlessly between vanity and self-loathing, apathy and resentment, resignation and rage. It's as sly as a snake, as cunning as a fox, and as charming as the devil. It will seduce you with as many lies as necessary to keep you in its grip."

I told him that, if this was his idea of a motivational speech, it needed work.

He chuckled. "Don't be ashamed of your fear, John. It's not a sign of weakness. Actually, it's a sign that you're paying attention. Fear is a rational response to the world you perceive through your shallow perceptual window: a world of constant change and tumult, everyone isolated from each other and in competition with each other, a battle of all against all to see who can collect more things that they don't really want or need. Eastern religions call this superficial rendering of the world "Maya," a veil of fear-laden thoughts that taints everything you see. But from where I'm standing, your fear doesn't look like a veil. It looks more like the walls of a dungeon."

I pictured myself trapped inside a dungeon whose walls were made of fear. The image made me shudder.

"Breaking free from that dungeon isn't easy," he said. "Your fear runs deep, and it hides itself well. You'll have to flush it out in all its guises before the doors of your perception will be washed clean."

I wrote a note in the top margin of a new page. *Flush out my fear.*

Wayne studied the note for half a minute, then said, "Fear is too broad a subject for one day. Let's break it down into three parts. First, identify the source of your fear. Second, examine how your fear develops. Third, uncover the remedy for your fear."

I added three lines to my previous note, my flush-out-my-fear to-do list.

FLUSH OUT MY FEAR

1. The source of my fear
2. Cultivating my fear
3. The remedy for my fear

I focused on the first entry, *The source of my fear.* I had no idea what that meant, so I sat in my chair and waited for Wayne to begin today's class. He made half a dozen laps of the room, walking fast and rubbing his chin. Finally, he stopped beside my desk and looked at me. His opening line took me by surprise.

"How is your digestion doing today?"

Excuse me?

"Your digestion," he repeated. "Is it going well, or is our conversation distracting you from it?"

I said nothing, baffled.

"My point is this," he said with a grin. "You don't control your digestion directly, it's an automated response programmed into your body. You control your digestion indirectly, by deciding what kind of foods you eat. Eat well, and you will feel well. Eat poorly, and you will feel poorly."

That made sense, but I didn't see how it applied to my perception.

"The same theory holds true for your perception," he said. "You can't control your perception merely by changing what you're thinking about. That's like trying to control your digestion after you've eaten a meal. To truly control your perception, you must go below your thoughts to your deeper psychological programming."

My deeper psychological programming. That sounded a lot like a computer's operating system.

"That's a great way of looking at it," he said. "Your thoughts operate on the surface of your psyche, like apps on a computer. A deeper programming runs beneath these apps, regulating them from below. I want you to consider the idea that you have two operating systems programmed into you, one designed to elicit emotions that fall along the spectrum of love, the other designed to elicit emotions that fall along the spectrum of fear."

It was an alluringly simple idea, two spectrums of psychological energy, like the AM and FM bands on a radio. Love denoted the upper bandwidth, fear the lower. In every moment, we radiate on a frequency that falls along one of these two bandwidths: the spectrum of love or the spectrum of fear. I loved this idea, and I told him so, but it brought up another question. What determines which operating system gets booted up at any given moment?

"Great question," he said. "That is determined by your answer to one key question that everyone is subconsciously asking in every moment of their lives: *Is the environment around me friendly or hostile?* Perceive your environment as friendly, and you will radiate on the spectrum of love. Perceive your environment as hostile, and you will radiate on the spectrum of fear."

I'd heard a variation of this idea before. It was attributed to Einstein and was often cited by spiritual teachers. I think I know why. Because it touched people on a primal level. But the question of whether we perceive our environment as friendly or hostile raised another equally important question: *On what level of our psyche do we make this determination?* My initial thought was the mind, but that didn't seem right to me. Living things were sensing threats long before the brain developed. It's logical to assume then that life's threat detector couldn't be located there. Sure, our mind helps us analyze threats and respond to threats, but our mind doesn't detect threats. That responsibility falls to our soul. Our soul determines whether the environment around us is friendly or hostile. And so our soul determines whether we live in peace or in fear.

My spiritual wingman flashed an exultant grin. "The soul pulls the strings of the mind," he said. A moment later, he was gone.

I flipped over a blank page and began to write.

LESSON FIVE

THE SOURCE OF OUR FEAR

"You have but two emotions, love and fear."

—A Course in Miracles

"You can't escape your fear until you know the full extent of your fear."

—John Dyer

PROGRAMMED INTO EACH of us are two operating systems, one designed to evoke emotions that fall along the spectrum of love, the other designed to evoke emotions that fall along the spectrum of fear. I call these operating systems 'peace mode' and 'panic mode', and they are two sets of physiological responses that are triggered inside us depending on whether we feel in our soul that we are alone or part of a larger group.

In evolutionary terms, it can be summed up like this: *Are you part of a herd, or are you alone in the wilderness?*

Before we begin, let's define terms.

Herd. Not a collection of physical bodies but a collection of spiritual energy, a gathering of aligned souls. When living things come together for a shared purpose, their psychological energy amasses like superposing waves. Connected to this amassed energy, we feel strong, secure, and content. Disconnected from this energy, we feel weak, insecure, and afraid.

Isolation. Not a physical separation but a psychological alienation, a separation at the level of the soul. The soul measures strength by the presence of love. If our soul feels love around us, it assumes we are part of a herd, and it puts us at ease. If our soul doesn't feel love around us, it assumes we are alone in the wilderness, and it puts us on our guard.

Love. Not the sensual love we feel in our body, but the divine love we radiate in our soul. Divine love has nothing to do with physical attraction, only spiritual acceptance. It's the embrace of others without initial conditions or judgment.

Peace mode is our natural psychological state. In peace mode, we feel safe, and our natural instinct is to open ourselves up. We are easy-going, generous, curious, optimistic, and trusting. Everyone is seen as a potential ally.

Panic mode is our defensive state, the inner fortress we retreat to when we feel threatened. In panic mode, we feel vulnerable, and our natural instinct is to withdraw. We become guarded, cynical, angry, and suspicious. Everyone is seen as a potential threat.

Ideally, we would all live in peace mode for the greater bulk of our lives, activating panic mode only when we face an actual threat. Unfortunately, this is not the case for most of us. Most of us live predominantly in panic mode, activating peace mode only for brief moments of peace and joy when our external circumstances align themselves right.

This seems like a backward way to live. And it *is* backward. But there is a good reason for it, and it goes back to our internal programming, specifically how our fear response is triggered. It doesn't take an actual threat to activate panic mode inside us, only an act of judgment. The simple act of being scrutinized is all it takes to put us on our guard.

To illustrate this, imagine that you are standing in front of a large crowd about to deliver a speech:

> *You stand at the podium and gaze out at the audience: hundreds of strangers staring at you, examining you, assessing you, judging you. Your soul senses this scrutiny and interprets it as a pack of predators stalking you. Immediately, it sounds the alarm.*
>
> *Battle stations.*
>
> *The human body operates much like a battleship, which, when not engaged in combat, operates as a floating village. The ship's crew maintains that village, performing necessary functions like cooking, cleaning, and making repairs. But the moment the captain sounds the alarm, everyone drops what they're doing and prepares for battle.*

Panic mode is the biological equivalent of battle stations, and as you face the crowd, you are firmly in its grip. Adrenaline courses through your veins, altering every system in your body. Your heart rate quickens, your breath shortens, your palms begin to sweat. Your physical senses heighten, making you hypersensitive to noise or movement around you. Your thoughts race, making you manic, impulsive, and flighty. You are thinking faster, but you can't concentrate on anything.

Rattled now, you take a series of deep breaths, trying to gather your thoughts. As you do, the audience grows impatient. Another wave of scrutiny hits you, and your symptoms intensify. Your heart beats harder, your thoughts whirl faster, your breaths come so short you can hardly breathe. Panicked now, you try to start your speech, but in a moment of sheer terror, you realize you can't remember the words. You've spent weeks memorizing this speech. You've practiced it a dozen times in front of a mirror. You could recite it in your sleep. But here, in the grip of fear, that same speech is an incomprehensible blur.

Your only thought now is escape. You want to run for the nearest exit, hide behind the podium, cover your face with your hands. Anything to get out of the spotlight of attention focused on you.

Now, ask yourself, why would you, or anyone else, be afraid of speaking in front of a crowd? Is your life being threatened? Are you in danger of bodily harm?

No. You are simply being judged.

The feeling of it can be as frightening as death itself.

JUDGE AT FIRST SIGHT

"Most of us are waging a nonstop internal mental skirmish with everyone we encounter."

—Dr. Wayne Dyer

"Anything short of love is a sign of hostility to the soul."

—John Dyer

Built into each of us is a finely tuned threat radar that can pick up the energy signature of being scrutinized. The moment another living being judges us, we sense it. And we respond to that judgment by putting up our guard.

This sensitivity to judgment is not a trait we learn, it's an automated response programmed into us over millions of years of evolutionary adaptation to environmental adversity. In a hostile environment, the ability to sense threats is an essential survival trait. Ask a fighter pilot, and they will tell you that the winner of a dogfight isn't the pilot with the fastest plane or the biggest gun but the pilot who sees the other guy first. That's why jet fighters are programmed to sound an alarm *not* when a shot is fired at them but when an external radar is locked onto them. By the time an adversary fires a shot, it's too late.

A similar programming exists inside us. Our internal alarm sounds *not* when another person attacks us, but when another person locks their internal radar onto us. The moment we feel we are being judged, we prepare ourselves for conflict.

Ironically, this sensitivity to judgment only goes one way: outward. Though we are keenly aware when others judge us, we are largely oblivious when we do the same to others. And yet most of us do it all the time. We like to think of ourselves as accepting of others, tolerant, forgiving. But if we examine ourselves closely, we often see that our initial response to other people is often laced with judgment. The moment we observe another person, our mind is already identifying their weaknesses, probing them for potential avenues of attack.

The greater bulk of this judgment is mild and can be best described as mental sniping. *"She's had more work done on her than the Statue of Liberty. I wonder how many Big Macs it's been since she actually fit into that dress she's wearing?"* These mental digs may seem harmless. After all, we aren't saying these things, just thinking them. But to those on the receiving end of our mental jabs, our hostility is plain as day. The soul reads intentions, not words. When we judge another person, we project a hostile energy pattern toward them. That person senses our hostility and responds by subconsciously jabbing back at us. We, in turn, sense *their* hostility, which to us seems unprovoked, so we subconsciously jab back at them.

This exchange takes place in seconds, long before any words are exchanged. We're like two boxers meeting at a pre-fight stare-down. The relationship starts out from a place of mutual distrust. Usually, it never recovers.

We don't treat each other this way because we are cruel. We treat each other this way because we are afraid. We've come to accept our judgment of others as normal because we've come to accept our fear as normal. And from our mind's perspective, fear and judgment *are* normal. Our brain has adapted to the hostile environment. The problem is, our soul never follows suit. The soul never dies, and the soul never settles. It wants love and nothing less. And so, as our mind continues to send out judgment to others, our soul continues to desire love back in return.

And we are constantly disappointed.

Again, it's vital to recognize that this cycle of fear and conflict originates in our soul not our mind. Ralph Waldo Emerson said that the ancestor to every action is a thought. Go one step deeper and you will discover that the ancestor to every thought is spirit. Ultimately, it's the state of our soul that determines the state of our mind, not the other way around. When our soul feels excluded from the living things around us, it concludes that we are vulnerable, and it prepares us for conflict.

Battle stations.

Over time, this perpetual state of high alert exerts a heavy toll.

DEATH BY A THOUSAND WORRIES

"Convinced of our separateness, we view life as a competitive exercise. The competition

> *increases the feeling of separateness and fosters anxiety about our place in the world."*
>
> —Dr. Wayne Dyer

> *"Fear is toxic at any dosage."*
>
> —John Dyer

In marshalling energy to confront an impending threat, the human body suppresses all internal functions not conducive to dealing with conflict. Returning to the analogy of a battleship, imagine if that ship's crew never left their battle stations. The ship would eventually break down from a chronic lack of maintenance. This is exactly what happens to us under prolonged stress. We perpetually divert energy away from the bodily functions that promote growth and recovery to the bodily functions that promote protection. Over time, our lack of internal maintenance causes us to break down.

Symptoms of chronic stress include heartburn, insomnia, heart palpitations, and ulcers. Another symptom is fatigue. Energy originally slated for reserves is instead burned directly. It's like an internal turbocharger that never turns off. We experience quick bursts of energy, but our fuel reserves quickly run out. We go from being able to deadlift twice our body weight to not being able to get out of bed in the morning.

The psychological effects of stress are equally toxic. Adrenaline in our brain alters our perception, shifting our awareness from the center of our attention to our periphery. In a hostile environment, this hypervigilance of our flanks is an effective survival mechanism, but in our daily lives, it induces a form of ADHD where our attention is constantly diverted from what we are trying to focus on to any and all distractions around us. In this hypervigilant state, we can be conversing with someone without registering a word they say. Likewise, we can be reading a textbook without comprehending a single idea. Our anxious mind, having determined that these activities are not a threat, is searching for threats elsewhere.

Irrational as our fear response is, it's extremely difficult to constrain. Evolution has built it into our internal programming. Our mind, in a state of fear, focuses on what is wrong in our environment, not what is right.

Have you ever caught yourself noticing only the things that go wrong during your day? Like when you're driving somewhere in a hurry, and you catch a red light, and you curse your bad luck for having caught it, even entertaining the idea that the light saw you coming and turned yellow just to spite you. Now, you may have sailed through a dozen green lights before hitting the red one, and you may sail through a dozen green lights after it, but the only light you reacted to was the one that didn't go your way. This is your mind in panic mode, seeking out negative patterns in your environment, filtering out everything else.

Once you recognize this negative behavioral pattern, you can see it crop up in your daily life. At work: *'I knew my idea would get shot down.'* On the road: *'I knew that jerk was going to cut me off.'* Even in your kitchen: *'I knew the wine opener was going to be in the last drawer I looked in.'*

You aren't pointing out facts here; you are filtering reality, blocking out everything around you but problems.

That's the worst part about panic mode, it's proactive. Once triggered, it starts identifying threats *before* they arise.

This goes back to our primordial programming, the fear response hard-wired into our DNA. In a hostile environment, we can't afford to wait for a predator to jump out from the shadows. By then it's too late. To survive, we must learn to fear the very shadows themselves.

Unfortunately, this is a skill we learn all too well.

A NEW STRAIN OF FEAR

"Fear is our prison."

—Dr. Wayne Dyer

"We are made to deal with mastodons, not minutiae."

—John Dyer

The long-term effects of stress are devastating: depression, hypertension, heart disease, and high blood pressure. Human beings aren't designed to live in fear for extended periods, even mild forms of it. Work deadlines, performance reviews, IRS audits, traffic jams—they are all relatively new phenomena, at least by evolutionary standards. We haven't had time to adapt to them yet. Big threats we can handle, but when faced with an endless succession of small stuff, we are defenseless.

It doesn't help that, in the background of our personal dramas, our culture is promoting fear as a high virtue rather than a deadly disease. Fashion designers peddle fear of aging. Drug companies peddle fear of diseases. The news media peddles fear of tragedies big and small. Even our education system peddles fear. The fear of graduating without a marketable degree.

Fear has become a must-have accessory in our lives. It's in our workplaces, in our homes, in our schools, and in our social gatherings. To be successful, we must live in perpetual fear. Eventually, it catches up with us, this living in opposition to our soul. Our anxiety builds slowly, like seismic energy gathering inside tectonic plates. The force goes unnoticed until it reaches a breaking point. Then our whole world starts to crumble.

At this point, the world becomes a place of hostility, and we live like soldiers trapped behind enemy lines, constantly surveying our perimeter for potential attacks. Ironically, this same hypervigilance that protected us from the mortal threats in the ancient world actually causes the mortal threats in the modern world: heart disease, addiction, depression, and suicide. We literally scare ourselves to death, one imagined threat at a time.

Ultimately, everyone realizes that stress is a serious disorder.

The question then becomes, how do we get rid of it?

THE CURRENTS THAT CARRY US

It's 1979, and I'm sitting in the front row of the Ford Auditorium in downtown Detroit, watching Wayne deliver a speech.

His life has changed dramatically since the day he pulled out of our driveway with every remaining copy of *Your Erroneous Zones* stowed in the car's rear compartment. The book, which his publisher wanted to stop printing at six thousand copies, has now sold more than six million copies. Wayne is an international celebrity, appearing regularly on national television, including *The Tonight Show*. His fame is surreal to me, but also intoxicating. I feel a sense of importance just being near him.

Wayne's appearance in Detroit is a homecoming for him. He grew up on Detroit's east side and attended college at nearby Wayne State University. During the lecture, Wayne speaks of his childhood, difficult times when their family was separated from each other. The boys' father walked out on his family when the boys were very young, forcing their mother to split them up so she could work to support them. My father was sent to live with his grandparents. David and Wayne were sent to a series of foster homes and orphanages. Their separation from each other lasted almost a decade.

I'd heard this story several times before, and it always made me feel grateful for having a father who was always there for me. Wayne continues his lecture with another story from his past, this one about a chance encounter between him and my dad when they were both in the Navy. It's a story about synchronicity, and I'd never heard it before. As I listen to it, I'm amazed.

It's mid-winter, 1959. Wayne is stationed in Lexington Park, Maryland. My dad is stationed in Norfolk, Virginia. It's Friday night, and both men have a weekend pass. Both are hitchhiking home. They haven't spoken to each other in months.

By 3 a.m., Wayne has made it to a service plaza along the Pennsylvania Turnpike, where his last ride had dropped him off. The temperature is well below zero, so Wayne grabs a hot chocolate at the plaza restaurant before heading out to catch his next ride. He wears a dark blue navy pea coat, its collar turned up against the driving wind.

Unbeknownst to Wayne, my father was dropped off at this same service plaza half an hour earlier and has been thumbing at the road without success. Now he's headed back to the restaurant to warm up.

As the two brothers pass each other on the freeway entrance ramp, neither one recognizes the other, but my dad sees the other man's navy uniform and warns his fellow sailor not to stay outside too long for fear of frostbite. Wayne thanks him and continues toward the road.

Twenty minutes later, the cold drives Wayne back into the restaurant, which is deserted now except for the other sailor. In the light, the two brothers recognize each other. Both are amazed by this seemingly impossible chance meeting.

As they catch up, a trucker pulls into the plaza to gas up. The boys ask the man where he's headed, and he tells them, "Toledo." Upon hearing their story, the man insists on taking them all the way to their house in Detroit, an hour out of his way.

I've heard this story half a dozen times since then, and it never fails to give me the tinglies. Something about this seemingly chance encounter points to a higher power at work in our lives, an "angelic co-pilot," as Wayne would say. I believe that a current runs through the fabric of all living things. This current is the force that drives salmon back to the stream where they were spawned, butterflies back to the forest where they were hatched, and soldiers back to their homes. When we align ourselves with this celestial current, we become part of a divine collaboration. Events will conspire to take us where we want to be.

After finishing this story, Wayne points out my dad in the audience, and all eyes momentarily turn our way. Later in the speech, I hear my name mentioned. Wayne is telling a story about me. What it's about, I don't know, but I imagine it has to do with sports.

I am wrong.

"When John was seven," Wayne announces to the crowd of several thousand, "I asked him what he wanted for Christmas, and he told me a tampon. This answer surprised me, so I asked John why he wanted a tampon. He said he saw it on TV. With a tampon, you can go swimming, hiking, horseback riding, and camping."

The audience roars. I go numb.

"John is here tonight," Wayne says as he points me out in the crowd. A woman to my left comments how "cute" that is. A man sitting behind me claps me on the back. My brother, sitting two seats down, is grinning from ear to ear.

The laughter fades, and the speech resumes, but for several minutes, I hear nothing. My only thought is that, in the mind of two thousand people, I will forever be known as The Tampon Boy.

For the first time it occurs to me that having a famous uncle might not be all it's cracked up to be.

DAY SIX

The rising sun glinted off the gold-tinted glass of a nearby skyscraper, catching my eye. I glanced at it momentarily, then returned to my editing. Writing the last section had opened my eyes to the full extent of my fear. Two days ago, if you had asked me if I was a fearful person, I would have answered, *Not since I was five.* Now, I saw the truth. I was more fearful now than when I was five. My fear had transformed since then. It had lost its fangs, but at the same time, it had grown roots. Fear was no longer something I had. Fear was now something I was.

"Good point," Wayne said, startling me from behind. I jumped in my chair, and spun around to face him, commenting snidely that the habit of sneaking up on people might be a reason ghosts had a bad reputation. Wayne laughed as he moved to the side of my desk.

"Can you picture yourself when you were five?" he asked.

I thought of a photograph that sat on my bookshelf: me, my brother, and my sister playing in the sandbox behind our house. My brother and sister knelt side-by-side in the sand. I stood on top of them, with one foot on each of their backs. The three of us made an unsteady pyramid, and as the picture was snapped, we were collapsing. I'll never forget the look on our faces as we tumbled to the sand: the laughter, the joy, the enthusiasm. Our grinning teeth shined bright white against our dirt-covered faces.

Yes, I told him.

"Good," he replied. "Now, try to imagine how you felt back then?"

I closed my eyes and tried to recall the feeling of that day. Several words came to mind: innocence, wonder, enthusiasm, serenity. But they were only words. I opened my eyes and shook my head.

No.

"Why not?" he asked.

The long-term effects of fear, I guess.

"Yes," he said. "Now tie that in with what you wrote in the last section."

I thought for a moment. Every human emotion falls within one of two psychological bandwidths: the spectrum of love or the spectrum of fear. Which spectrum we radiate on depends on whether we feel in our soul that we are part of a larger community or not. If our soul feels connected to the living things around us, we radiate on the spectrum of love. If our soul doesn't feel connected to the living things around us, we radiate on the spectrum of fear.

"Great summary," Wayne said. "Now let me ask you this. What happens when the communities people create are themselves a source of fear?"

I gasped as I heard this. Such a simple idea, yet it explained so much, namely why fear remained so prevalent in modern society despite the fact that most people lived in relatively safe communities. Because the communities we create aren't sanctuaries of acceptance and love, but asylums of judgment and fear.

Wayne gazed out at the city. His expression reminded me of a medic overlooking a war-torn battlefield. "So much needless suffering," he lamented. "People living in communities that provide neither security nor fulfillment. Everyone gathered together and yet isolated within themselves."

The disturbing image returned of a dungeon inside me: a dark place, hidden deep inside me, where I hid from the constant judgment of the world.

"That's good," he said as he turned toward me. "You're seeing your fear more clearly now. Don't shy away from that image, disturbing as it may be. Look your fear straight in the eye. Only then will you realize how unsubstantial it is."

I closed my eyes and tried to picture my psychological dungeon. I saw myself standing on a bare stone floor, cold and damp. Surrounding me was a swirling wall of fear, like the eyewall of a hurricane.

"Yes," Wayne murmured as though picturing the image himself. "At the bottom of that eyewall lies fear's darkest incarnations: self-loathing, panic, hopelessness, and despair. Higher up is anger, rage, hatred, and hostility. Above that, resignation, indifference, cynicism, and doubt. At the top, greed, ambition, arrogance, and pride."

Wayne's gaze had gradually risen as he described the levels of fear. He was now looking at a spot high on the wall behind me.

"Most people spend their lives climbing the walls of their psychological dungeon, trading one form of fear for another. They feel insecure, and they counter it with arrogance. They feel inadequate, and they counter it with greed. They feel apathetic, and they counter it with aggression. They feel resignation, and they counter it with ambition. Relatively speaking, higher expressions of fear feel better than lower ones. Arrogance feels better than insecurity. Greed feels better than inadequacy. Aggression feels better than apathy. Ambition feels better than resignation. But no form of fear is truly satisfying, so they never stop climbing. They're always striving but never arriving."

Wayne let out a breath. His expression was equal parts compassion and dismay.

"People climb the walls of their psychological dungeon in hopes of escaping it, but their efforts are in vain. The higher they climb along the walls of their fear, the steeper those walls become. Eventually, they fall back down. Arrogance reverts to insecurity, greed reverts to inadequacy, ambition reverts to apathy." He turned toward me. His eyes were glistening. "Some people never stop this cycle. Others simply give up. They stop climbing the walls of their psychological dungeon and just lie down on its floor. This is depression, when you quit fighting your fear and just resign yourself to it."

I took notes for several minutes. When I was done, I looked them over. My spiritual wingman had painted a bleak picture, but I knew this wasn't the end of the story. Fear is our disease, not our destiny. Like all diseases, it can be cured. The question was how?

Wayne flashed a hopeful grin. "The way to free yourself from your psychological dungeon is to examine how it was created in the first place. It didn't start out as a dungeon."

What then?

"A fortress."

This was my morning of aha moments, and here was another. We don't build our psychological dungeon in order to imprison ourselves. We build our psychological dungeon to protect ourselves. Just as our body responds to physical wounds by hardening our skin, our psyche responds to psychological wounds by hardening our perception. It's like a perceptual callus we build around our soul. A fortress of dead perception that shields us from the pain of a love-starved world.

I flipped open a new page and began to write. Wayne whispered one last line. "We are damned by our defenses." And he was gone.

LESSON SIX

CULTIVATING OUR FEAR

"One does not become enlightened by imagining figures of light, but by making the darkness conscious."

—Carl Jung

"Fear is a habitual response lodged in the subconscious mind from early childhood."

—Dr. Wayne Dyer

"We are compelled to love but conditioned to fear."

—John Dyer

FOR THE FIRST six months of our lives, the world sees us as we truly are: bundles of joy, perfect little miracles that need only food, sleep, and love. But as we get older, that gradually changes. No longer are we seen as gems to be treasured but as vacant land to be developed. Like land, we are measured, analyzed, compared, and valued. The moment this evaluation process begins, we start to withdraw.

Have you ever wondered why babies are so happy? It's because no one has judged them yet. No one calls a baby short, fat, dumb, or clumsy. No one mocks them when they drool on themselves, wet themselves, or tip over randomly like drunken sailors. The truth is, for the first few years of our lives, everyone loves us for what we are. For the remainder of our lives, everyone judges us for what we are not.

Now, this isn't to say we shouldn't try to improve ourselves. Human beings are made for learning, aspiring, and accomplishing. But what we aren't made for is subsisting without love. And yet our culture seems to be founded on this very principle. It's as though we've collectively determined that love is like milk, something we need only for the first few years of our lives. At the age of five, the time for love is over. Now it's time to "make something" of ourselves.

In school, our development focuses almost exclusively on our mind. Facts, figures, and equations are fed to us on a non-stop assembly line. *2+2=4. I before E except after C. The capital of France is Paris.* Over time, our education instills in us two deep-seated beliefs. First, that life is a series of problems to be solved. Second, the more problems we solve, the more successful we will be.

Both are illusions.

If only our schools expended as much time and energy on filling their student's souls with love as they do filling their students' heads with facts and figures, how much happier, healthier, and more peaceful we would all be. But sadly, this is not the case. Public schools avoid the subject of divine love altogether. Parochial schools present love within the context of their particular religious doctrine. In neither case is divine love considered a language, like grammar or math, that must be universally adopted in order for society to function properly. Words and numbers teach us how to communicate, but divine love teaches us what to communicate. Without fluency in each, everything we learn will be tainted by fear.

Look closely at our education system and you'll see that it's founded on fear. Students who make the grade are rewarded. Students who don't are punished. We call this approach "carrot and stick," but it's really all stick, for the driving force behind the reward and the punishment is the same. Fear. Low-achieving students fear being deemed a failure. High-achieving students fear being deemed anything less than the best. Everyone is judged constantly, and they learn by example to do the same. No one is immune to this disparagement because everyone's criteria for what makes them better than others are their own. Smart kids judge others by grades. Athletic kids judge others by sports. Wealthy kids judge others by possessions. Attractive kids judge others by looks. Everyone's standards are different, but the end result is the same. We are all judged constantly, and because of it, we all withdraw.

Each of us has a psychological fortress inside us that we retreat to when we feel threatened. This fortress doesn't exist at our birth, we build it gradually throughout our lives, brick by brick. Each time we are judged, criticized, mocked, ridiculed, or betrayed, we add another brick to the wall around our soul. We call this process "withdrawal," but that's a misnomer really. We aren't retreating inward. We're retreating outward. This makes sense when you think about it. The source of our suffering isn't pain from the outside.

The source of our suffering is emptiness from the inside. That's what we're shying away from, not life itself but our unadulterated connection to life, which is our soul. We withdraw to our surface to avoid feeling deep pain.

By the time we reach adolescence, most of us are already experiencing symptoms of our growing isolation: loneliness, anxiety, insecurity, and longing. And just then, our body goes haywire. Adolescence is an awkward time for most. We feel ugly at the very time we most want to feel attractive. Our need for love has not diminished. And yet, as the pace of our lives accelerates, we are feeling love less and less. School is more demanding, our parents more critical, our peers more competitive. It seems that the closer we get to adulthood, the less we learn about what is right with us and the more we learn about what is wrong.

By high school, most of us have experienced both numerous crushes and numerous crushed hearts, and we find ourselves in the perplexing state of being simultaneously attracted to each other and petrified of each other.

Neither our parents nor our teachers seem overly concerned about our plight. "*There will be time for love later,*" they assure us. "*For now, focus on grades, test scores, extracurricular activities, sports... anything that looks good on a college application. Look good on paper, and you will feel good in your life.*"

But for most of us, our high school years are fraught with insecurity and self-doubt. We see love paraded all around us, in books, magazines, movies, and songs. Seeing love everywhere, we naturally assume that everyone else is experiencing it. But since we ourselves are not, we conclude that something must be wrong with us, that we are unlovable for some reason.

That's when we start finding faults with ourselves. *If only I was beautiful. If only I was smart. If only I came from money.* What we fail to recognize is that everyone feels insufficient, even those who seemingly have it all: looks, talent, brains, and money. None of us feel fulfilled, because none of us are getting enough of what we really want, acceptance of who we are. We are all love-starved, and because of it, we are all constantly judging everyone, including ourselves.

This relentless judgment only validates our insecurities, driving us further into our psychological shell. Eventually, we lay the last brick around our soul, and our inner fortress is complete. And that's when we discover something truly terrifying. It's not a fortress we've created, it's a dungeon. Our defenses haven't insulated us from our pain. Our defenses have actually encased us within it. The pain is still there, it has simply morphed from something sharp and temporary to something dull and permanent.

We've literally locked ourselves inside our fear.

YOU ARE THE LIGHT

It's April 2015, and my 3 a.m. wake-up calls are entering their fifth month. Every morning, it's the same routine: wake up before sunrise, write down the ideas that have taken up temporary residence in my head, and then deposit my notes in a box underneath my desk.

At first, this seemingly miraculous phenomenon inspired me. But over time, doubts began creeping in. A part of me remained convinced that I was being guided by a higher power. But another part of me—my rational side—concluded something else.

That I was wasting my time.

My rational side had a point. Writing was taking a toll on me, both personally and professionally. My business had suffered, and my social life was virtually non-existent. I'd moved to Denver to enjoy the outdoors: hiking, biking, and skiing. But I'd spent the greater bulk of my time sitting in my apartment scribbling notes on scraps of paper.

And honestly, what was I going to do with these notes? Assemble them into a book? I knew the harsh realities of the publishing business. The odds of a book being published were slim. Slimmer still were the odds of that book being successful. And here I was writing about a subject I knew almost nothing about. What were the chances that anyone would want to read it?

Virtually none.

On the night of April 23, 2015, my rational side won the debate. I decided to quit my position of unpaid spiritual transcriber and return to my safe routine. As a symbolic gesture, I stashed my box of notes in my bedroom closet, hidden behind my golf bag (another unprofitable avocation I had recently given up). I wanted to send a clear message to the universe. *The homeless shelter for misfit spiritual musings has closed its doors in Denver for good. Find someone else to haunt.*

Afterward, I felt good about what I'd done. The empty space beneath my desk represented freedom for me. I could refocus on work I actually got paid for, and start enjoying the activities Colorado had to offer.

For two days, I managed to suppress my soul. Then, on April 25—the day Wayne came to Denver to speak at a self-empowerment conference—the lid blew off my soul for good.

It began on the morning of Wayne's speech. I awoke at 7 a.m., after eight hours of blissfully uninterrupted sleep, and decided to go for a run. I entered my bedroom closet to fetch my running shoes. And that's when I saw it. My golf bag had been moved. Behind it was the bare wall.

My box of notes was gone.

I stepped out of the closet and looked across the room. There it was, back underneath my desk. I approached the box slowly, as one might advance towards a ghost. When I stood over it, I noticed a sticky note affixed to the top of the stack. Written on that note were four neatly penned words.

I scanned my bedroom, looking for what, I don't know, perhaps signs of an intruder who had broken into my apartment to move my box of notes and then write me an inspirational note. Of course, I knew I had moved the box myself. But the thing is, I've never sleepwalked, nor have I ever forgotten waking up to write, even if it was only one line.

Stranger still were the words themselves. The handwriting was mine, but the message seemed foreign to me, like it was written by someone else. I probed my memory for some train of thought that could have led me to this idea but found nothing.

I didn't have time to dwell on this mystery. I had a busy workday ahead of me before I attended Wayne's lecture that evening. And to be honest, everything about me was a bit 'off' at that point. So I sleepwalked. Who cared? Maybe tomorrow, I'll wake up to discover that I'd cleaned my apartment in my sleep. Like my grandfather once said, "Forgetting stuff is underrated."

The day passed uneventfully, and at 7 p.m. I was pulling into the parking garage of the Denver Convention Center. I brought a friend with me who was a fan of my uncle, and as we waited in our seats for the lecture to begin, she asked me about the four large poster boards that were laid out on easels across the stage. I explained to her that the poster boards were visual aids. Each board had a message displayed on it that was concealed by a flip-up cover. Wayne would uncover the messages one by one as the lecture progressed.

"What do you think they say?" she asked.

I have no idea, I told her. Let's wait and see.

The house lights went down, and Wayne began his lecture. After a short introduction, he approached the first poster board.

"I'll be speaking about a new subject tonight," he said, "one that I'm planning to write a new book about."

The news of a new book surprised me. A year ago, Wayne had announced to his family that he was retiring from writing. I'm not sure anyone believed him when he said this. Writing was as much a part of him as waking up in the morning. But now his unofficial retirement was officially over. Dr. Wayne Dyer was going to write his forty-second book. I was anxious to hear what it was about.

Wayne flipped over the cover. My breath left me in a rush.

You are the light.

The same four words from the sticky note in my bedroom. Words that seemed to be written by someone else, and that I couldn't trace to any train of thought. It all made sense to me now: the cardboard box that had moved itself, the sticky note that had written itself, the message on the poster board that matched the sticky note word for word. This was no cosmic coincidence. This was a message from Wayne, delivered soul to soul.

You are not alone. And you can't give up.

The remainder of the lecture was mostly a blur to me, but I do remember how Wayne ended it:

> "There is a part of your life clock, from six to twelve, that I call living in the light. This will be the subject of my next book. I'm gathering notes now. I will begin writing when I return from my worldwide tour."

After the lecture, I waited backstage to see Wayne, but I never got the chance. He had a flight to catch that night. After signing autographs, he left for the airport.

I never saw him again.

Back home, I sat on the side of my bed, staring expectantly at my box of notes. I'm not sure what I was expecting from it, perhaps a heavenly light to burst forth, illuminating the room. Nothing emerged. As I climbed into bed, it occurred to me that the ideas in that box were waiting for a heavenly light to burst forth from me. I chuckled at the thought as I turned off the lights. In the darkness, I wondered if such a light existed inside me. And, if so, how could I turn it on?

I received no answer from the universe. And that was okay with me. I didn't need to see the light just then, just a light at the end of the tunnel. I had that now, and my resolve returned. I would have faith in my higher navigator. Faith in the understanding beyond my rationale. Faith in the light that connects us all.

I believe that Wayne knew well before his passing that his time in his earthly incarnation was short, and that if his message was to continue unfolding, a new outlet for his celestial source of inspiration would have to be recruited.

I can picture him presenting my business card to his angelic co-pilot.

> "This is your new contact. His name is John, and he lives in Denver. Yes, he'll listen when you send him messages. And yes, he's just crazy enough to drop everything in his life to write it all down."

The next morning, my 3 a.m. wake-up calls resumed. The cardboard box never again left its spot under my desk.

DAY SEVEN

When my spiritual wingman arrived the next morning, I was already at my desk, reviewing the last two chapters. In general, I was pleased with them. My goal had been to flush out my fear from the shadows of my perception into the light of day. I had succeeded at that. Unfortunately, exposing my fear hadn't dissolved my fear, as I had secretly hoped. My fear remained firmly planted in my perception—cool, confident, defiant. *'Now that you see me,'* it taunted, *'what are you going to do about it?'*

It was a good question. I had no doubt what the remedy for fear was. Priests, prophets, and poets all agreed it was love. What I couldn't figure out was how to administer that remedy. Given the fact that our mind, in a state of fear, is actively filtering out all non-threatening activity, where does that leave the most non-threatening activity of all: love? How can we flush out the fear in our mind when that same fear is blocking love from coming in?

"You bring up an important point," Wayne noted, beginning today's class. "I once wrote that love dissolves all negativity, not by attacking it, but by bathing it in higher frequencies, much as light dissolves darkness by its mere presence. I was speaking here of divine love, not intellectual love. Love in the soul versus love in the mind."

I considered the idea of two versions of love. It seemed wrong to me. I recalled the Bob Marley song: *One Love.* That felt right to me. This did not.

"Your instinct is correct," Wayne said. "There is only one true version of love, but that doesn't mean there aren't imposters. Do you remember when I told you that the things you see around you are a reflection of how you see yourself?"

Yes.

"Well, love is no exception. When you see yourself from your soul's perspective (as integrally connected with everyone else), your definition of love reflects this connectivity. It becomes inclusive. But when you see yourself from your mind's perspective (as separate from everyone else), your definition of love reflects this separation. It becomes exclusive. Your mind will try to convince you that exclusivity is good. "Save your love for those who deserve it," your mind will proclaim. But your soul knows the opposite is true. The more selective you are with your love, the less chance you have of experiencing it. Take this exclusivity to the extreme by saving your love for one special person who is "made for you," and you have a good chance of never experiencing it at all."

I made a note. *Love that is exclusive is love that is scarce.* I held it up for Wayne, and he smiled.

"Intellectual love is a form of exclusion," he said. "It's you deciding who is worthy of your affection and who is not. Divine love is the polar opposite, the acceptance of others without initial conditions or demands. Two versions of love, one real, one an imposter. One the antidote for fear, the other just another form of fear."

I made another note: *Divine love is the light of our being. Intellectual love is nothing but noise.* I showed it to Wayne, but this time he didn't smile.

"You've reached a crossroads," he said with a forbidding tone that made me take note. "You recognize that love is the cure for fear. That's good. But knowing the cure isn't administering the cure. Your fear runs deeper than you think. It penetrates the very pores of your perception. Everything you see is tainted by it, including your definition of love."

It disturbed me to think that love could be twisted into its opposite, like a t-shirt turning inside out in the wash. I looked at my spiritual wingman. His blue eyes, normally warm, were now ice cold. "It's time you took a hard look at your own definition of love," he said. "You just may discover that it's nothing but noise."

I shuddered as he said this, and suddenly I wasn't so eager to start writing this morning. I waited for Wayne to leave me so I could do just that—write. But he kept staring at me with those cold, piercing eyes.

"What are you waiting for?" he pressed. "Ask yourself what you love."

Right now?

"Yes."

I closed my eyes and asked myself what I loved. Immediately, my mind shot back a response. *Other people.* Now, normally I would have accepted this answer, but not this time. The words had rolled out too fast, too smooth. It reminded me of the artful movement of a pickpocket.

"You asked the wrong question," Wayne remarked coolly. "You can't be vague when you ask yourself a tough question, or your mind will find a way to evade it. So ask the question again, and this time be specific."

The specific definition of love? I looked at him blankly.

Wayne said nothing at first, then leaned in toward me and whispered in my ear. As he pulled away, he began fading into the sunlight. "Answer this question honestly," he said as he faded, "and you will discover what you truly love. And why you've spent so much of your life in fear."

A moment later, he was gone.

It was just me in the room now, me and the question Wayne had whispered to me. I hesitated a moment, as though a part of me didn't want the question answered. Then I took a deep breath and recited his words verbatim.

This time, there was no prepared response from my mind. In fact, it was stone silence in my head for quite some time. Finally, an answer emerged... slowly, gradually, like a crocodile rising out of a slime-covered swamp.

I sat at my desk for several minutes, staring into space. Then I picked up a pen and began to write.

LESSON SEVEN

THE REMEDY FOR OUR FEAR

"You need to examine your fears with honesty and with love. When you do, you will transform your fears with love into love."

—Dr. Wayne Dyer

"True love is defined not by what you desire but by what you value."

—John Dyer

WHAT DO I love?

When I first asked myself this question, my mind shot back its prepared response: *other people*. This was the feel-good answer I wanted to hear, but it wasn't the honest answer. The honest answer arrived when I asked the question Wayne had whispered to me. Sharp, piercing, and brutally direct, his words left no place for me to hide.

"What do you accept without judging, pursue without reasoning, hoard without needing, and appreciate without understanding?"

The moment I spoke these words, it became obvious what I truly loved. Not people but possessions. I accepted possessions without judgment, pursued them without reason, hoarded them without necessity, and appreciated them without understanding.

I did none of these things with other people.

This was perhaps the most important realization of my life, for it revealed how my sense of value had turned upside down. I treated people like possessions and possessions like people. I appreciated possessions for what they were. I judged people for what they were not.

My initial reaction to this revelation was shock. How had my definition of love become inverted without me even knowing it? It made no sense. I knew full well that the pursuit of material things was futile. I'd seen it fail in my own life, and I'd seen it fail in the lives of countless others. In fact, I truly believed that no one had ever attained true happiness by collecting material things. Love is the only real precious gem in the universe! I knew this. What's more, I actually believed it. And yet I continued to act as if the opposite was true. I continued pursuing the very things I knew had no value. I had become a hoarder of things and a user of people.

Exactly the opposite of what we were intended to be.

OUR SHALLOW AND DEEP PERSPECTIVES

> *"At any given moment in your life, you are choosing between two pictures or evaluations of yourself."*
>
> —Dr. Wayne Dyer

> *"We are either lovers or hoarders."*
>
> —John Dyer

Human beings seek connection from the first moments of life. There, in the delivery room, as we cry our first tears, it isn't positive affirmations from the medical staff that soothes us: *"Turn that frown around, kiddo, today is the first day of the rest of your life."* No, we are soothed by human touch, the loving embrace of our mother. Connection is what we seek, what we crave, what makes us whole. In the first five minutes of our life, we discover our true purpose. Our soul never forgets it. Our mind never stops looking for bigger and better things.

During our early years, our soul remains our primary perceptual vantage point, and we reflect its energy. We are open, trusting, outgoing, and enthusiastic. We understand nothing and appreciate everything. Life is a miracle to explore.

But as we get older, our awareness gradually shifts to our mind. As it does, we begin to take on our mind's traits. We become cold, calculating, covetous, competitive. We understand everything and appreciate nothing. Life becomes a series of problems to be solved.

By the time we reach adulthood, most of us have developed two opposing worldviews: the shallow view of our mind and the deeper view of our soul. Neither of these worldviews is right or wrong, nor is either good or bad. Both try their best to serve us. They simply do so from different points of view.

Our mind sees our physical body as our life form. The preservation and expansion of that life form is our mind's purpose. In fulfilling this purpose, our mind compels us to consume, collect, and compete. This makes sense from our mind's point of view, for our mind sees a world of separate and sovereign physical beings competing with each other for finite material resources. In this world of perpetual scarcity, possessions are the measure of self-worth. Everything we possess enlarges us. Everything we share diminishes us. The value of human beings is measured by their utility. If a person assists us in expanding our net worth of things, they are valuable. If not, they are useless.

This is the worldview of our mind.

Our soul sees a very different world. From our soul's perspective, all living things share the same life force. The preservation and expansion of that life force is its purpose. In fulfilling this purpose, our soul compels us to preserve, share, and collaborate. This is logical from our soul's point of view, for our soul sees us as an interconnected spiritual being living in an infinite world of shared energy. In this world of unlimited abundance, relationships are the measure of self-worth. Everything we possess diminishes us. Everything we share enlarges us. The value of material objects is measured by their utility. If an object assists us in expanding our net worth of relationships, it is valuable. If not, it is useless.

This is the worldview of our soul.

We take on the traits of the perceptual level we connect with. If we see the world from our mind's perspective, we are driven by fear to collect. If we see the world from our soul's perspective, we are driven by love to connect.

We can see this as a choice if we like. And from our mind's perspective, it is a choice. But from our soul's perspective, there is no choice, for our soul knows something that our mind does not.

Our mind can't be satisfied.

When we perceive the world from our mind, we reflect its energy. And we take on its trait of perpetual dissatisfaction.

OUR INSATIABLE FORM

> *"You can never get enough of what you don't really want."*
>
> —Dr. Wayne Dyer

> *"It's the curse of selfishness. The more we practice it, the less effective it becomes."*
>
> —John Dyer

Human beings instinctively sense that their possessions don't fulfill them. We often refer to our possessions as "toys," and yet we can't seem to stop collecting them. Why? Because we are addicted to them. We don't really want these things so much as we are afraid of not having them. Without them, we have nothing to distract us from the deeper pain we feel from a chronic lack of love.

The truth is, the human mind has no capacity to be fulfilled. It's a tool of fulfillment, not a source of fulfillment. And it's an amazing tool when used for that purpose. The human mind has an unlimited capacity to imagine, reason, design, and build. And yet most of us squander that tool by using it primarily for the purpose of collecting more tools.

To illustrate this, imagine that you're shopping for a new house in an undeveloped subdivision. This subdivision has no sales office. There are no renderings to look at, no floorplans to review, just rows of undeveloped lots with construction materials piled on them.

Which lot would you choose?

The one with the biggest pile, of course.

This is exactly how most of us fabricate our life, as a never-ending construction project. Unable to grasp our true design or purpose, we embark on a life of unbridled accumulation, perpetually adding more stuff onto our pile. To a mind unguided by a deeper spiritual purpose, this seems like progress. But it isn't, and here's why. All physical desires are a form of appetite, much like our hunger for food. We all know that eating a meal doesn't end our hunger forever. In a few hours, when the food is metabolized, we will be hungry again. Our body understands this concept. Our mind, however, is not so wise. Our mind is convinced that the new car we just financed over seventy-two months will enthrall us for each and every day of that term. But it won't. Our mind metabolizes the car just like our body metabolizes food. The car is like candy for our brain. It feels good while we are consuming it, but the satisfaction quickly fades as our brain digests it.

And we become hungry for more.

This is the nature of all physical desires, the hunger grows in equal proportion to how much we feed it. Feed our body more food, and our stomach will expand to match it. Feed our mind more possessions, and our desire will expand to match that as well. Whatever we attain becomes the foundation of our next desire in a never-ending quest for more.

No physical thing is immune to this psychological metabolism, not fame, fortune, power, or prestige. All are psychological snacks that quickly pass through us. Deep down, none of us really want this psychological junk food. What we really want is love. But not knowing how to get it, we settle for cheap emotional substitutes like possessions, power, drugs, and status. We're like starving people eating rotten food out of a dumpster. Spiritually, we are so hungry that we settle for rotten psychological sustenance.

This is how addictions are born. We hunger for love in our soul, and we try to satisfy that hunger by overfeeding our physical form. These efforts are not only futile, they are actually self-destructive. When we strive for things that we don't really want, we can never get enough of them. Eventually, our perpetual striving overtaxes us. Physically and mentally, we begin to break down.

Escape from this trap is simple. Stop chasing things you don't really want. Once you understand what you really want, you won't have to chase it.

It will come to you.

THE LAW OF ATTRACTION

> *"You do not attract what you want. You attract what you are."*
>
> —Dr. Wayne Dyer

> *"When more is what you want, want is what you get."*
>
> —John Dyer

Imagine a world where human beings could attract material objects with their mind.

> *You stand on the corner of a busy city intersection, waiting for the lights to change so you can cross the street. Half a dozen people wait with you on the corner. Half a dozen more wait on the corner across the street. Suddenly, an armored truck enters the intersection and makes a hard right-hand turn in front of you. Halfway through the turn, the truck's rear doors fly open, and a gold bar falls out. The bar clanks to the ground and tumbles across the pavement, coming to rest at the center of the intersection. Everyone on both sides of the street is staring at it.*
>
> *Immediately, everyone focuses their attention on the gold. "I want that gold... I deserve that gold... The universe OWES me that gold." The gold bar rises ghostlike off the pavement, lurching first toward one person, then another, then someone else. It's caught in the sway of a dozen mental tractor beams, a real psychic standoff. Finally, a man with his eyes closed and his arms spread out wide gathers sufficient psychic energy to break the gridlock. The gold bar hurtles toward him like a cannon shot. It strikes him in the chest, killing him instantly.*

Be careful what you wish for.

The law of attraction is a real phenomenon. We can and do attract the energy we radiate, but it's not the energy of our thoughts that we attract, it's the energy of our spirit. Whatever energy our soul radiates attracts more of that energy.

Now, this isn't to say that obsessing over money won't help you make more money. It likely will. What I'm saying is that the money you fixate on won't satisfy you. Just the opposite. When you obsess over money, you don't produce more prosperity, you produce more obsession. Why? Because that is what your soul perceives. Your soul can't perceive money. It has no receptor in it for material things. Your soul senses the obsession. This, then, is what you get more of: obsession, want, hunger, and lack.

This explains why a great many wealthy people remain unfulfilled despite their riches. Their coffers are full, but their soul remains empty. Ultimately, our experience of life is determined not by what we see with our eyes or what we think with our mind but by what we radiate in our soul. If our soul is full, our life is full. If our soul is empty, our life is empty.

We will never be truly happy until we recognize that possessions aren't what we really want. What we really want are the feelings of abundance, security, and freedom.

These feelings don't come from collecting things. They come from giving things away.

TO GIVE IS TO RECEIVE

"Possession is proved only by giving. All you are unable to give possesses you."

—André Gide

"Service to others is fulfillment for yourself."

—John Dyer

To our mind, the idea of giving things away seems illogical, but to our soul, it makes perfect sense. When we give something away, we are sending ourselves a message that we have more of that thing than we need. Our soul receives that message and responds by triggering the physiological responses that make us feel content. I say again, the mind is a tool of fulfillment not a source of fulfillment. It has no concept of "enough." Our mind waits for our soul to signal to us that we've had enough of something. And our soul does this only one way, by seeing us share that thing with others.

Honestly, the universe is doing us a favor when it denies our prayers for material things. By failing to manifest our shallow desires, the universe is sending us a message. THIS ISN'T WHAT YOU REALLY WANT! Listen to it. Our true net worth isn't determined by how much stuff we have in our closets but by how much love we have in our soul.

It takes a long time for most people to accept this notion. Some never do. But look closely at anyone who is truly happy, and you will discover their secret.

Your attachment to belongings imprisons you. Your service to others sets you free.

THE REAL DEFINITION OF LOVE

> *"We must raise ourselves to the levels of energy where we are the love we feel is missing. By being it, we attract it to us."*
>
> —Dr. Wayne Dyer

> *"Love is not made for us. We are made for love."*
>
> —John Dyer

Love is the miracle drug of the universe. It both satisfies the hunger in our soul and eases the fear in our mind. Deep down, everyone knows this, which is why we seek love in the first place. We want to experience the peace, joy, and fulfillment that only love can provide. We search for love constantly, but rarely do we find it. We think it's because we are looking in the wrong place, but it's really because we are looking for the wrong thing.

Our soul sees love as an obligation, a responsibility we have to others to accept them without initial conditions or demands. Our mind sees love as something else, not a responsibility but a right, one special person who is "made for us" and will fulfill our needs forever. This notion of a made-to-order soulmate makes perfect sense from our mind's perspective, for our mind sees everything from a superficial vantage point, and a soulmate is the superficial definition of love. It's an alluring idea. Unfortunately, it isn't real. Psychologically speaking, there is no such thing as superficial love. There is only divine love, and there is fear. This explains why so many people live their lives predominantly afraid. They're constantly trying to heal real fear with fake love.

And it doesn't work.

The moment we see love as something we get rather than something we give, we embark on a hopeless path of trying to attract it to ourselves rather than producing it for others. We've all been down this long, lonely road of fishing for a soulmate. Like bait on a line, we try to make ourselves more alluring. Makeup to look nicer. Cologne to smell nicer. Jewelry to reflect the sunlight and catch the eye of a potential suitor. We don't engage in this flurry of self-embellishment in order to deceive other people, we just want someone to love us. Unfortunately, our efforts are in vain. By appealing to the shallow nature in other people, we invoke that very nature from them, the very part of them that is incapable of producing the love we so desperately crave.

Many supposedly loving relationships are really nothing more than physical attractions in disguise, not the meeting of two loving souls but the meeting of two fearful minds. We don't enter into these relationships because the other person is right for us. We enter into these relationships because we ourselves feel so wrong. So hungry are we for love that we attempt to wring it out of anyone, no matter how incompatible they may be for us. But a relationship based solely on physical attraction is destined to fail. The relationship may gratify us physically and pacify us psychologically, but it won't satisfy us spiritually. Therefore, it won't last. Eventually, we metabolize the other person like a piece of psychological candy. The thrills fade while the drama builds. At some point, the relationship snaps like an overstressed tree branch, and we are off in search of the next reprieve from our emptiness.

We play out this drama over and over, with different partners but with the same underlying dysfunction and the same eventual outcome—conflict. It's a universal law, those who aren't spiritually connected to each other will end up in conflict with each other. We are either actively loving one another or passively competing with one another. There is no in-between.

THE BEAUTIFUL PEOPLE

Over the years, my cousin Tracy and I attended many of Wayne's lectures. As we did, we noticed a change in the makeup of his audience. As his message became more spiritual, so did the people who came to hear him speak. In the 70s and early 80s, Wayne's lectures resembled cocktail parties. Men wore suits, women wore dresses. By the late 80s, Wayne's lectures looked more like a Grateful Dead concert. You still saw suits and dresses, but you also saw flowing skirts, sandals, tie-dye shirts, and even saris.

These latter types were the "New Agers," an eclectic group of spiritual practitioners who took swatches of wisdom from a variety of religious and secular sources and stitched them together into a kind of spiritual quilt. My cousin and I called them "The Beautiful People" on account of their tendency to use the word 'beautiful' a lot. People were beautiful. Nature was beautiful. Traffic was beautiful. EVERYTHING was beautiful. The beautiful people smiled a lot, and they liked to dance, sometimes even when no music was playing. They stared at things for a long time, as though seeing the world through an inner kaleidoscope. I secretly suspected that some of them were high on some drug.

"So you're Wayne's children?" a woman asked us after one of Wayne's lectures. Wayne was signing autographs at the front of the stage. Tracy and I were sitting in our seats in the front row. The woman wore a long, flowing dress and brown suede sandals. She held a copy of *You'll See It When You Believe It* under her arm.

"I'm his daughter," Tracy said. "This is his nephew."

The woman smiled at us sweetly. "Your father is very special," she said. "He helped me through a difficult time in my life."

"Tell him that when you see him," Tracy told her. "He'd love to hear your story."

The woman nodded, then stared at Tracy as though examining a work of art. "You have his eyes," she remarked. "Beautiful blue." The woman turned to me next, but apparently couldn't find anything noteworthy to point out. I decided to help her out.

"I didn't get his hair."

The woman chuckled, then turned to check the autograph line. A dozen people still waiting. She turned back to us, still smiling.

Tracy noticed the woman's necklace, a long silver chain adorned with so many beads and amulets that it jingled when she walked, like a spiritual cowbell. Tracy said she liked it.

"Thank you," the woman beamed. "That's a beautiful thing to say."

Tracy and I looked at each other, trying not to laugh. The woman continued smiling at us as though relishing a sip of fine wine. It was uncomfortable but not unpleasant. I can't say I related to the beautiful people, but I liked them.

After a few minutes, the woman left us to join the autograph line. "Namaste," she said and walked away.

The moment she was out of range, my cousin and I broke into our shtick. I grabbed a crumpled foil gum wrapper from my pants pocket and presented it to Tracy in cupped palms. "A gift for you," I said. "I made it myself."

She cooed. "That's beautiful."

"You're beautiful for saying so," I responded.

"How beautiful of you to notice."

I gazed at her dreamily. "Your eyes make sapphires weep. If the ocean saw them, it would no longer call itself blue."

Tracy batted her eyelashes. "Oh, these old things, I suppose they're nice. Sometimes I cry just so my tears have a chance to see them."

"How considerate of you."

This continued for many minutes. Eventually, we ran out of beautiful things to say to each other and just waited in silence for Wayne to finish signing autographs. On the ride back to our hotel, we replayed our act for Wayne. He wagged his head at us, but he laughed all the same. He had a sense of humor about everything, including himself. This, I believe, is why so many people related to him. He never considered himself to be an ascended master, just another traveler along the path. Like everyone, he stumbled sometimes. This didn't make him disingenuous. This made him real.

I picture him now as a tour guide in the afterlife for beautiful people who have recently passed. He rides in a retired school bus that has been painted over with images of flowers, rainbows, and peace signs. Ram Dass drives. Wayne stands in the aisle, microphone in hand, pointing out celestial celebrities:

On our left is Rumi playing a board game with Albert Einstein. I can't see what they are playing, but if it's chess, my money's on Einstein. If it's Scrabble, Rumi.

"Up on the right is Buddha jogging beside the road. Look how fit and trim he is. No more lazing under a Bodhi tree for the Enlightened One, he is running four miles a day. He's got his earbuds in, probably listening to his favorite band: Nirvana.

"We're approaching heaven's homeless shelter now. That's Mother Theresa standing at the front entrance. See how she's smiling? Can anyone guess why? Because the shelter is empty. Heaven's homeless shelter is empty.

"Oh, now here's a treat. Carl Jung and Sigmund Freud are taking a walk. Looks like they're engaged in a lively conversation. I wonder what they're debating? Collective consciousness? Dream interpretation? The role of spirituality in psychology? Needless to say, Freud's skepticism of the afterlife has been greatly diminished.

"Shush now, we're passing St. Francis napping beside the road. A flock of ducks have perched on him to keep him warm."

DAY EIGHT

Wayne arrived the next morning at his usual time, as the sun peeked out over the horizon. Sunrises mesmerized him. He would gaze at the morning sky like an art lover gazing at the roof of the Sistine Chapel. "Look," he would blurt out as he pointed to some section of the sky: a cloud formation, a color pattern, a shadow moving across the mountains. I would look to where he was pointing, stare at it a moment, nod politely, then return to my work. I envied him the way he found such wonder in ordinary things. I wished that, for one moment, I could see the world through his eyes.

Done with my editing, I gathered the marked-up pages and added them to the manuscript tray. As I did, my spiritual wingman turned to me.

"Another piece of the puzzle," he announced cheerily. "Each day, the picture becomes clearer. Each day, you draw closer to the light."

I looked at him skeptically. Actually, I was thinking the opposite, that my book about discovering my inner light was growing kind of dark. I understood the concept of flushing out my darkness before I could see the light, but after three days of peeling away layers of my fear, I was starting to wonder if the process would ever end.

"Don't get discouraged," Wayne said. "It's normal to feel this way."

Normal? I countered. Normal to be questioning your life's path when you are this far down it?

"Especially then," he insisted. "When you are attempting to make a life-altering change, you will always feel the urge to quit at the very moment you are about to succeed. It's a last-ditch effort by your fear-conditioned mind to keep you in its grips. Do you remember when I told you that you were like a caterpillar that didn't know it was a butterfly?"

Of course. Who can forget being compared to an insect?

"Well, now you're like a butterfly that still believes it's a caterpillar. Your soul is ready to take flight, but your mind is still telling you that it's too dangerous to fly."

I pictured my mind as an overprotective mother warning me not to play outside for fear of skinning my knees.

"Your mind still sees your soul as weak and irrational," he said. "It will continue to try to protect you from it under the guise of keeping you safe. Don't listen to it. You are closer to your goal than you realize."

I wanted to believe him. And yes, I did feel I was making progress. But I still didn't feel enlightened. I could see the light, but I still couldn't *be* the light.

"You're still missing an essential piece of the puzzle," he said.

Which is?

"Power," he said, then began to pace. "A few months ago, you wrote an essay titled *Our Higher Power.* Do you remember it?"

I did. I wrote that the concept of a higher power is found in all cultures. It's known by different names in different places, but every culture seems to agree on one thing: to tap into a higher power, we must first relinquish a lower one.

Nodding, Wayne said, "I've often written about the higher force of the universe. The force that effortlessly controls our digestion, respiration, circulation, and metabolism at once. The force that created life from stardust, minds from globs of protoplasm, love, compassion, honor, and hope from vibrating strings inside atoms. This force exists within you, but its power source does not, any more than the power source that lights a lightbulb exists inside the lightbulb itself."

The power grid of life, I commented.

"I like that image," he said as he passed behind me. "All living things wired together in one universal energy grid. Physics tells us that low levels of power produce weak fields of energy, while high levels of power produce strong fields of energy. This theory holds true for all forms of energy, from light bulbs to human beings. In light bulbs, more power produces more light. In human beings, the effect is the same. The more power we tap into, the brighter we shine."

I pictured myself driving down a remote country road on a moonless night. With the low beams on, I drive cautiously. But with the high beams on, I drive confidently.

"Another good image," he said. "Your perception is the light that illuminates your world. When that light is bright, you feel strong and secure. When that light is dim, you feel weak and afraid."

I imagined myself as a lightbulb that radiated personality, a walking, talking beam of light. I had a low-wattage version of myself that radiated dread, doubt, and fear. And I had a high-wattage version of myself that radiated hope, faith, and love. A dark self and a light self. I loved the analogy, but it raised another question: How do I switch between my two inner incarnations? My car has a lever on the steering column that toggles the headlights between the low and high beams. Where is the toggle inside me that switches between my light and dark self?

"Your consciousness," Wayne answered without hesitation. "When you see the world through your shallow perceptual window, you tap into your weak source of energy, and you manifest your dark self. When you see the world from your deep perceptual window, you tap into your strong source of power, and you manifest your light self."

Three images entered my mind simultaneously: an energy cell inside me, a power grid above me, and an electrical cord hanging from my hip that I could plug into either one.

Wayne pressed his palms together and bowed toward me, then he turned toward the window to make his exit. It was still early morning, and the sunlight that washed over him was hazy, filled with golden streaks. He leaned into the sunlight like a bodysurfer leaning into an oncoming wave. Gradually, he faded into the light, like a drop of water returning to the ocean. One moment, he was there, the next, he was everywhere.

"Show off," I said, then turned my attention to the blank page in front of me. I thought about harmony and alignment, and an invisible electrical grid that connected all living things. Then I thought about light. The light we produce when we are connected.

I felt the pen in my hand move toward the paper. I set it to the page and watched it go to work.

LESSON EIGHT

OUR HIGHER POWER

"Your ultimate choice is whether to align yourself with a high energy field or a low energy field."

—Dr. Wayne Dyer

"In form, we are shells. In spirit, we are batteries. In union, we are light."

—John Dyer

EACH OF US has access to two sources of energy: an internal power grid that fuels our physical form, and an external power grid that fuels our spirit.

Our internal power grid consists of a network of nerves, veins, and tissues that run throughout our body. The energy flowing through this grid powers our bodily functions: digestion, perspiration, circulation, and metabolism. We fuel this power grid with food and water.

Our external power grid consists of a network of all living things. The energy flowing through this grid powers our higher psychological states: our sense of peace, purpose, enthusiasm, and fulfillment. We fuel this power grid with divine love.

We connect to these two power grids through shifts in our consciousness. Picture consciousness as a power cord that can be plugged into multiple sockets. When we see ourselves from our shallow perspective (as a separate and sovereign physical being), we plug into our internal power grid. This manifests our dark self. When we see ourselves from our deep perspective (as an interconnected spiritual being), we plug into the power grid of life. This manifests our light self.

OUR DARK SELF

> *"The primary energy that you have been using all your life is life-sustaining but does not provide the sense of fulfillment and bliss that we long for."*
>
> —Dr. Wayne Dyer

> *"A sinner is nothing more than an underpowered saint."*
>
> —John Dyer

Our dark self is the low-wattage version of us. It's us shining dimly, our personality radiating like the low beams on a car. Everything around us looks bleak, everyone we meet seems sinister. This gloomy outlook isn't the result of a personality disorder, it's the result of a personality power deficiency. We are operating on only half our available energy.

This deficiency affects all aspects of our being: our outlook, our impulses, our emotional responses, even our physical strength. Spirit is like a turbocharger for our personality. Without it, we feel insecure, unsatisfied, and afraid.

Many people refer to their dark self as their "inner demons." I prefer to call it our inner prisoner. It's us trapped within the artificial boundaries of our own shallow perception of ourselves. I say again, our self-image is self-fulfilling. Whatever we see as our psychological boundaries *become* those boundaries. If we see ourselves as separate from other people, we become separated from them. We yank the plug out of our soul, so to speak. Our inner light extinguishes, and our personality goes dark.

Immediately, our dark impulses take over, and we feel the urge to consume, collect, compete, and control. This is how our dark self gets energy, by stealing it from others. It's the only means of empowerment it knows. To our dark self, life is a competitive venture, satisfaction a zero-sum game. To feel better ourselves, someone else must feel worse.

Everyone has experienced the rush of dark energy. We call it the thrill of victory, and it does feel momentarily good. But if we examine that thrill closely, we see how fleeting it is. The exhilaration is so brief, in fact, that the moment we "win" at something, we immediately feel the need to either disparage the loser or boast about our victory to others. We've already metabolized the victory, and are now seeking a second psychological boost by reliving it in our mind. That's the problem with dark energy, it's psychological snack food. The high comes quickly, but it passes just as fast. When we rely on dark energy for our psychological sustenance, we must consume it constantly.

Paradoxically, those who radiate their weak energy are sure to believe they are strong. Their insecure mind has convinced them that they are in control, large and in charge. They believe they are the king of their castle when they are really the warden of their own prison.

TRUE POWER

> *"Defining empowerment only in material world terms is a reflection of being spiritually disconnected."*
>
> —Dr. Wayne Dyer

> *"When a drop of water rejoins the ocean, it has all the powers of its source."*
>
> —Dr. Wayne Dyer

> *"True power doesn't move mountains. True power eradicates fear."*
>
> —John Dyer

Most people equate power with physical force. Muscles equate to strength. Knowledge equates to wisdom. Possessions equate to wealth. Logical as these statements sound, they ultimately ring hollow. Bigger muscles can lift more objects, but that doesn't make us stronger. Greater knowledge can solve more problems, but that doesn't make us wiser. Working harder can earn more money, but that doesn't make us richer.

We live in a psychological world, *not* a physical world, and psychologically speaking, power can only be measured one way: by the absence of fear. This is why love is considered the most powerful force in the universe, not because it can move physical objects but because it's the remedy for the one force that truly weakens us—fear. Fear is the great pickpocket of the universe. It will steal the satisfaction out of everything we try to consume, collect, or control. Whatever we gain will never be enough. Always, there will be another battle to fight, another trophy to win, another possession to attain. We will never feel secure or content.

True fulfillment comes only one way, by filling the empty space inside us. And the only way to do that is to connect with other living things.

OUR LIGHT SELF

> *"There is something much bigger than you, something you're always connected to..."*
>
> —Dr. Wayne Dyer

> *"It's through others that we either find or love our self."*
>
> —Dr. Wayne Dyer

> *"The more living things we connect with, the more powerful we become."*
>
> —John Dyer

The truth is, none of us have the capacity to produce love on our own. On our own, we simply don't have the power. Many people will balk at this notion. They were taught to believe that they must first love themselves before they can love others. The opposite is true. We can't love ourselves until we first love others. Without the energy of others, our own inner light will not ignite.

Quite literally, we turn each other on.

Picture yourself as a flashlight that is powered by multiple batteries. Your soul represents one battery in that flashlight. Next to your soul are empty slots that are made for more batteries. As long as those slots beside your soul remain empty, your inner light will remain unlit, and you will live in fear. Those empty slots can't be filled with food, drugs, power, or possessions. They can only be filled by the spirit of other living things. Two or more batteries creating one collective light.

The psychological states that everyone longs to experience are all products of this collective energy: inspiration, enthusiasm, gratitude, joy, purpose, contentment, serenity, and bliss. Never are these sensations the product of one individual. Always, they are the product of two or more living things aligning their spiritual energy.

People often say they want to find themselves. What they really mean is that they want to join a cause that is greater than themselves. They long to feel the peace, purpose, and passion that arise when we join with others toward a shared purpose. Our desire to feel this collective energy is so ingrained in us that, in its absence, we feel incomplete.

Of course, if our mind is unenlightened, we won't see things this way. We will view the act of surrendering to a higher cause as a sign of weakness. But our soul knows the opposite is true. Psychologically speaking, our most powerful mindset isn't seeing ourselves as better than everyone else. Our most powerful mindset is seeing ourselves as exactly like everyone else. When we see ourselves as better or worse than other people, we radiate on a different psychological frequency from them. Psychologically speaking, we cancel them out. At this point, we are operating solely on our internal energy, and we feel insufficient, insecure, and unfulfilled. Only when we see ourselves as equal to other people can we align our psychological energy with them. Only then will the light of love ignite between us. Only then will we feel strong, secure, and fulfilled.

But we can't align energy with others until we first align the energy within ourselves. And the only way to do that is to align our thoughts with our spirit. The opposite approach—aligning our spirit with our thoughts—will never work. Our soul can't be trained to be selfish, greedy, or uncaring. It wants love and nothing less. Our mind, on the other hand, can be trained to desire anything. It makes sense then that we should align the relative part of us to the absolute part of us. This means training our thoughts to be as selfless, humble, and empathetic as our soul.

The more everyone does this, the happier we will be.

The truth is, we aren't self-sufficient, we're self-deficient. Sure, we can survive on our own, but we can't fulfill ourselves on our own. We just aren't made for it.

We are spirit. We are made to love.

THE SON OF MAN

My parents viewed church the same way they viewed the dentist: two visits a year was sufficient. I didn't learn much from attending a decade's worth of Christmas and Easter services, just that Jesus was born, Jesus died, and Jesus resurrected. During one Easter service when I was six, I told my mother that Jesus was like a trick birthday candle because he came back to life. I thought it was a compliment. My mother told me I was blaspheming.

Over the years, I learned more about Christianity, including its depiction of the soul, which never really resonated with me. It reminded me of the flight recorders they installed on airplanes. Upon our death, angels swoop down, retrieve our soul, and deliver it to St. Peter, who reviews the transcripts and determines from it whether we spend eternity in heaven or hell.

This rendition of the soul was neither persuasive nor inspiring to me. As Einstein said, *"If people are good only because they fear punishment, and hope for reward, then we are a sorry lot indeed."*

That said, one aspect of Christianity did intrigue me: the message of Jesus Christ himself. One night I was channel surfing and I came across a movie depicting the life of Jesus. Now, normally the first glimpse of religious programming would send my thumb clicking the remote, but not on this night. This night, I decided to watch.

I tuned in as Jesus was delivering the Sermon on the Mount. This was nothing like The Ten Commandments, which was the only other religious movie I'd seen. There were no whirlwinds of fire, killer mists, or parting oceans, just a man on a hill speaking to a crowd of people. But something about his words captured me. *"Do not be anxious about tomorrow, for tomorrow will be anxious for itself." "Judge not, that you be not judged." "You are the salt of the earth. You are the light of the world."* There was power in his message. And wisdom.

Later in the broadcast, Jesus addressed a crowd of men preparing to stone a woman for adultery. The men asked Jesus what he thought of this practice. His reply was so simple, so beautiful, so brilliant.

"Let he who is without sin cast the first stone."

Chills coursed through me as I heard this. No unjust law could withstand the force of such raw and penetrating truth. I watched the men drop their stones one by one.

I continued watching, strangely engrossed by events that I knew only vaguely: the Last Supper, the Betrayal, and the Crucifixion. I found myself repeatedly amazed not only by the virtue of Jesus's words but by their strange, beguiling logic.

It culminated for me as Jesus languished on the cross. Flayed, impaled, and slowly suffocating, He delivered a final message to his persecutors.

"Forgive them Father, for they know not what they do."

Tears rolled down my cheeks as I heard this, shocking me with their presence. Why this man moved me so deeply, I couldn't say. His message made no sense. "*To give is to receive.*" "*Those who exalt themselves shall be humbled. Those who humble themselves shall be exalted.*" "*Bless your enemies. Do good to those who mistreat you.*" It was all backward, logic and reason turned on its head.

It was irrational. And yet it felt right.

I continued watching through the Ascension, which added little to the story for me. The power of Jesus Christ stemmed from the timelessness of his message not the timelessness of his physical form. He became immortal the moment He spoke it.

I think back to the day I compared Jesus to a trick birthday candle. I considered it a compliment then, and I still do today. The Man who ignited the light that will never be extinguished. The Carpenter whose message delivered us from the darkness of our own defenses.

DAY NINE

That night, I dreamt I was standing on the deck of an enormous suspension bridge. Thick mist swirled around me, obscuring my view of the bridge, but I saw enough of it to know it was deserted. No cars were in the traffic lanes, no people in the pedestrian walkway. I saw a support column ahead of me, a towering framework of metal plates and girders that rose around the deck and disappeared into the mist high above me. Steel cables hung down from it in neat rows. Where the bridge began or ended, I couldn't say. From where I stood, it seemed like a fixture of the sky itself.

It was a peaceful place, and for a moment, I just took it all in: the fresh air, the cool mist, the sound of the wind whistling through the cables. Then I heard a voice:

> *Consider all the components that come together to create this bridge. Now ask yourself which piece is most important?*

I glanced around me, considering my choices: the deck, the trusses, the cables, the support columns. Which one is most important? I really couldn't say. They were all indispensable. Remove any of them, and the bridge would collapse.

There was a break in the mist ahead of me, and in the clearing, I saw that the bridge extended beyond the horizon, as far as I could see. I wondered briefly where the bridge ended, then it dawned on me that it didn't matter.

> *Ultimately, life isn't about the destinations we reach, or the journeys we take, but the bridges we build. The ties that bind us are the wires that empower us.*

The wind died, and there was silence for a moment. Then this:

> *The moment people stop trying to determine who is most important amongst them is the moment humanity finally opens its eyes.*

And I awoke.

* * *

When I opened my eyes, it was well past sunrise. Wayne stood next to my desk, gazing up at the sky. Snow had fallen in the mountains during the night, and the higher elevations were draped in a shroud of brilliant white. I pushed a pillow to the headboard and sat up against it. My spiritual wingman turned to me and smiled.

"I want to tell you the story of how I found faith."

Okay.

"Like you, I was more of an agnostic, pragmatic kind of person. My attitude was that, if I couldn't see it, touch it, feel it, or smell it, then it didn't apply. Then I read a story where you were asked to imagine a cyclone hitting a junkyard full of aircraft components and randomly assembling the pieces into a working 747 airplane. From random rubbish to precise perfection by accident. As I contemplated the absurdity of this, I thought about how I once proclaimed such an explanation for the universe itself, with zillions upon zillions of component parts all arriving and interacting with each other in perfect symmetry. All just working out coincidentally, by sheer chance and happenstance. I revised my viewpoint to accommodate a newly arrived sense that there has to be a creative energy at work here."

I tried to imagine this creative energy. I pictured an electromagnet field running throughout the universe that arranged things into beautiful patterns, like metal filings gathering around a magnet.

Wayne nodded his approval. "I can tell you this much about what my new perspective has taught me. Nothing about the living world makes sense if you assume that its driving force is either chance or the struggle to survive. The living world only makes sense when you recognize that its driving force is love."

Love makes the world go around. A month ago, I would have laughed at the idea. Now I saw it for what it was: a living, breathing physical law.

"Evolution is a tale of collaboration, not competition," he said. "All living things are communities. These communities formed out of trust, not fear. Fear leads to withdrawal, withdrawal leads to isolation, isolation leads to conflict, conflict leads to extinction. This explains why some species survived while others didn't. Organisms that feared one another perished. Organisms that trusted one another survived."

Simple as this idea was, it absolutely floored me. It was the most amazing description of evolution I had ever heard. The species that ultimately survive aren't those that are strongest, or most intelligent, but those that display the greatest capacity for collaboration, the greatest capacity for love. This is why everyone is drawn to love. It's the impulse we feel most deeply inside us, the call of a billion years of life coming together toward a higher cause.

"Trillions of cells come together to form you," he said, his voice rising a notch. "Each one plays a part inside you that is so small their insignificance is beyond measure. What keeps them going in the midst of such staggering unimportance? Why don't they just quit?"

Wayne pointed at me and smiled. "Because they have faith in something greater than themselves. They believe in you. You are their higher purpose, but you are not your own higher purpose. You, too, are meant to play a role in something greater than yourself."

He looked out the window. The sky was cloudless, a deep, shimmering blue.

"There is a magic in our coming together," he said. "We aren't merely a collection of particles, we are a collection of miracles, one laid on top of the other."

I grabbed my notepad from the nightstand and wrote down his words, relishing each one. Wayne continued to gaze out at the city.

"Why can't people see that everyone is connected?" he mused. "Is it because they don't see wires running between us?

People believe that their cell phone can connect to a satellite. They believe that their computer can connect to a wireless network. So why don't they believe that human beings can connect with other living things?"

I thought back to what I'd written earlier about the power grid of life. I'd pictured that grid as a matrix of wires strung over everything, like the wires you see hanging over old streetcar tracks. That image, I realized, was wrong. Spiritual energy has no physical medium. It permeates the air like a Wi-Fi network, invisible to the senses but accessible to the soul.

Wayne turned around to face me. He was shaking his head and laughing.

"Only you could compare the divine energy of the universe to a coffee shop Wi-Fi network. I have to admit, though, it's a great analogy. A network of spiritual energy that your soul perceives like a cell phone detecting a Wi-Fi network. Everyone has the ability to connect to this spiritual network, but few ever do."

Why not?

"Because they don't have the connection key."

So, what's the key to connecting with other people? I asked.

Wayne turned toward the window and let out a breath. "Your faith in other people is your connection to other people. To tap into their power, you have to believe..."

Believe what?

"That they are a part of you."

I thought back to my dream of the bridge. It made more sense to me now. We are all components of a bridge made of souls. This bridge has no starting point, and no ending point.

Its purpose isn't to transport us somewhere. Its purpose is to elevate us above the darkness inside ourselves. This bridge is not made of concrete and steel. It's made of our faith in one another. Believe in that bridge, and it appears. Doubt it, and it collapses.

Wayne smiled contentedly. "That's the piece of the puzzle that sits at the center of it all, John. Faith is always first. Love arises from power. And power arises from faith."

LESSON NINE

FAITH

"The antidote to fear is faith."

—Dr. Wayne Dyer

"Only the ties that bind us together have the power to set us free."

—John Dyer

AT SOME POINT in your life, a wise guru taught you life's most important lesson. Chances are, you don't recall this incident. You don't remember the guru's name, nor the words of wisdom that guru imparted to you. And the reason is simple. That guru was a toddler, and they never said a word to you. The lesson they taught you was when they ran up and leaped into your arms.

Just about everyone has been love-mugged by a child. Maybe it was your own child, or a sibling's, or even a friend's. Regardless, have you ever felt so good as when you held that child in your arms? "*I missed you,*" they say as they press themselves against your chest.

Even if you haven't experienced a love-mugging yourself, chances are you've witnessed one. And you felt good just the same. You couldn't help it. Love is a detonation created by a synergy of spiritual energy. Everyone in the blast zone feels it.

Now, it's important to understand the mechanics of this love wave. It was the adult who produced it, but it was the child who triggered it. And how did the child do that? By trusting that the adult would catch them. Love is the light of the world, but faith is the spark that ignites it.

When people have faith in one another, a wave of love is produced between them. This love wave expands in all directions, infusing everyone it touches with a burst of inner sunshine. People often describe this sensation as "warming their hearts." This is an accurate description. Love is indeed felt in our hearts, but our hearts don't produce it. Love is the product of a divine collaboration between two or more aligned souls.

OUR MISPLACED FAITH

> *"When you change the way you look at things, the things you look at change."*
>
> —Dr. Wayne Dyer

> *"You don't really know someone until you trust them."*
>
> —John Dyer

The most common fears among children are darkness, high places, monsters, thunderstorms, and being alone. The most common fears among adults are public speaking, crowds, intimacy, failure, rejection, and commitment.

Notice how our fears change over time from inanimate things to people. This shift coincides with our perceptual shift from our soul to our mind. The older we get, the less trust we put in people and the more trust we put in material things.

It's amazing how much faith we place in machines. We'll climb into an airplane that takes us thirty thousand feet into the air without knowing the first thing about it. The same holds true for taxicabs, busses, subways, gondolas, even carnival rides. We implicitly trust machines while we implicitly distrust people.

Imagine if we treated machinery with the same skepticism that we treat other people.

> *We enter the lobby of a high-rise office building for an appointment on the tenth floor. We've never been in this building before, so when the elevator arrives, we don't just step right in, we check it out first to see if it's safe. We poke our head inside the cabin and look around. Immediately, we notice red flags. Water stains on the ceiling tiles, faded carpet on the floor, scratched faux wood panels on the walls. The elevator's operating permit says it's twenty-five years old, but it looks older than that in person. We've seen this trick pulled on online dating sites—an artificially enhanced profile.*
>
> *Suspicious now, we step back into the lobby and let the elevator make a round trip without us. As we wait, we pull out our phone*

> *and Google the building's address, searching for anything suspicious in its past. Two minutes later, the elevator returns to the lobby. Our online search has produced nothing, and now we see two people emerge from the elevator unscathed. So we enter the cabin and reach for the panel, but we don't take it to the tenth floor just yet. We make a trial run to the second floor since a fall from that height won't kill us.*

This example may seem ridiculous, but it illustrates where we put our faith, not in people but in material things. We assume machines are trustworthy until they prove themselves dangerous. We assume people are untrustworthy until they prove themselves safe.

This vigilance of strangers will no doubt seem prudent to some. "Bad people are out there," they will argue, "ready to take advantage of us the moment we let our guard down. Common sense dictates that we remain wary of others until they reveal their true intentions."

Here's the problem with that approach. Our scrutiny of other people won't reveal their true intentions, because our scrutiny of other people fundamentally alters their behavior. People who are being scrutinized are not authentic versions of themselves, any more than a caged tiger is an authentic version of a tiger. Our scrutiny of them fundamentally alters their behavior. Scientists call this phenomenon *The Observer Effect,* and it holds true for everything in the universe, from subatomic particles to human beings. People not only respond to how we look at them, they are partially defined by how we look at them.

Now, this isn't to say we shouldn't be wary of people who are actively threatening us. Fear is an appropriate response in that situation. But what we shouldn't do is assume that people are a threat. Assuming people are a threat helps make them a threat. When we prepare ourselves for conflict with others, we subconsciously invite that very response from them. We can't help it. It's just the way we are. When we change the way we look at people, the people we look at change.

Admittedly, no one has the time or energy to give their full loving attention to everyone they encounter, but everyone can meet others without judgment, and, in doing so, reveal their true nature. See others as brothers, not strangers. Make them prove they are a threat rather than the other way around.

Love first, ask questions later.

Those who consider this approach foolish are the real fools. A stranger isn't someone you've never met. A stranger is someone you've never trusted. No one is a stranger to a young child or a puppy. To them, everyone deserves to be treated the same: love-mugged.

Of course, everyone can cite instances when someone disrespected them without provocation. When this happens, ask yourself this: *Did I meet that person with sincere love or with thinly veiled indifference?* When you express indifference toward another person, don't be surprised if they respond with a stronger expression of fear, such as arrogance, resentment, withdrawal, or even anger. Fear begets fear and the trend is always downward. Likewise, love begets love, and the trend is always upward.

People will generally respond to you with the same energy that you meet them with. Send out love to others and they will return the same. But this divine alchemy only works if your love is sincere. Fake love may fool your mind, but it won't fool anyone else's soul. To spark the light of love in someone you have to genuinely care for them.

Ultimately, the condition of your world is determined by how you treat the next person that you meet. Are you excited to see them, genuinely interested in what they have to say? Most importantly, how do you see them in relation to yourself? Do you consider them an ally or an adversary? A treasure or a tool?

The only true gold in the universe is the golden rule. Treat others exactly how you yourself want to be treated. This is easy because everyone wants the same three fundamental things.

Regard. We all want to be acknowledged. Not merely noticed but welcomed, accepted, and appreciated.

Respect. We all want to be seen as valuable. Equals not inferiors, assets not obstacles, brothers not strangers.

Responsibility. We all want other people to look out for us, to see our welfare as part of their concern.

Of course, putting the golden rule into practice in a fear-dominated world isn't always easy. It takes great courage to be the first person on a psychological battlefield to shed their inner armor. You become an easy target for those who wish to inflate themselves by putting others down. Their barbs will sting, and your natural instinct will be to withdraw into your shell. Don't do it! Remember, it's not a fortress you're retreating to, it's a dungeon. Shakespeare's famous line about cowards dying many deaths while the valiant die just once has more to do with love than war.

> Our deepest fear is not of fighting one another.
> Our deepest fear is of truly loving one another.
> It's the vulnerability that can free us that frightens us the most.

That said, I'm not suggesting that we drop our defenses completely. I'm suggesting that we transform our defenses from protective armor to radiant light. We can find love anywhere, even on a battlefield. We just have to stop seeing ourselves as soldiers and start seeing ourselves as healers.

THE HEALER INSIDE US

> *"By you working at not having any judgments or harmful thoughts, those around you will be free of anguish."*
>
> —Dr. Wayne Dyer

> *"A little love makes you a sucker. A lot of love makes you a saint."*
>
> —John Dyer

See the people who treat you unkindly for what they are: prisoners, not persecutors. They aren't lashing out at you, they are lashing out at the walls of their own internal prison. If you came upon an accident scene and you found a victim cursing in pain, you wouldn't tell them to watch their language, you would try to help them. Do the same for people who trespass against you. See through their hostility to their underlying pain.

Remember, fear is contagious, and it will infect you if you allow it to draw you in. Don't get entangled with it. When someone sneezes next to you, you don't turn toward the germs and swat at them, you turn the other way. Do the same when others act unkindly toward you. Don't fight their fear, expose it to its opposing energy. Meet their fear with understanding, with compassion, with empathy, and with love. Don't forgive those who hurt you—there's nothing to forgive. People who are suffering cry out in pain. That's what they do. You don't forgive the sick for being ill. You try to heal them.

When you encounter a fearful person, picture yourself as a doctor treating a patient. Remind yourself that you are a healer, not a judger, part of the cure, not the disease. Remaining true to this vision will allow you to immunize yourself from their fear, and to remedy theirs.

You need no medical training to do this. When it comes to administering love, there is no such thing as a misdiagnosis. Love can't be misapplied, and it can't be over-administered. It's safe in all situations and at all dosages.

If others reject your love, it's only because you haven't broken through their psychological defenses yet. Don't stop trying! Love the doubt right out of them. Acknowledge them, respect them, value them. See them as an extension of yourself. When you treat others this way, they will have no choice but to love you back. Every cell in their body will respond to the force of your faith in them.

Love courageously, without expectation or judgment: no conditions, no stipulations, no demands. Don't save your love for those who deserve it, lavish your love on everyone you see. The more of it you give, the more you will get in return.

Love isn't reasonable, so don't try to be reasonable with it. Commit yourself one-hundred percent to loving the person in front of you. It's the only way to penetrate their inner armor, and to prevent you from donning yours. Believe in them with the same conviction that you believe in yourself. Do this and you cannot fail. Doubt them and you've failed already.

Each of us shares the highest responsibility in the universe, not to be the one who breaks the chain of love. Don't lose your faith in other people. Don't hesitate. Don't equivocate. Don't be afraid.

Love like there's no tomorrow.

Gandhi said, "Be the change you want to see in the world." This is another way of saying, *Be the love you wish to feel from the world.* Stop seeking love from others and start producing it for them. It's really that simple. Those who seek love never find it. Those who produce love never need to seek it.

You don't have to ponder this on a mountaintop or chant it in an abbey. You simply have to know it, because it is the truth. The key to self-actualization is self-realization. Know what you are and you will know what to do.

Don't think less. Don't feel less. Just love more.

Do this and the rest will take care of itself.

LESSON TEN

THE NAME OF SPIRIT

"We are all connected, there is an invisible force in the universe that pervades all life."

—Dr. Wayne Dyer

"It is not the label that matters. What's important is knowing that the intelligence is there and that it is a part of you and all life."

—Dr. Wayne Dyer

"Great stars die not in darkness but in their greatest display of light."

—John Dyer

OUR LAST DAY of class began like all the others. I was up before dawn, editing the last section. On previous mornings, Wayne would arrive as I finished editing. But not today. I was done with my edits, and Wayne still hadn't appeared. As I waited, I recapped what I had learned.

Dimensions. We are aware in three dimensions at once (sensually, rationally, and spiritually) and in two directions at once (proactively and reactively). Our consciousness connects to these dimensions like a radio receiver tuning into different stations. We adopt the aspects of the dimension of awareness we connect with. Tune into our mind and we are driven by fear to collect. Tune into our soul and we are driven by love to connect.

Power. We all have access to two sources of power: physical energy that flows through our physical form, and spiritual energy that flows through our soul. When we tap into our physical energy alone, we manifest our dark, frightened self. When we tap into the spiritual energy of others, we manifest our light, loving self.

Faith. Enlightenment doesn't come from believing in the light. Enlightenment comes from believing in the power source that produces that light: other people. The more faith we send out to others, the more love we receive in return. Knowing this, our goal should be to judge people on the lowest level possible and love people on the highest level possible.

Soul. The soul is the home within us that exists outside us. It's our foundation and our farthest reach, our road map and our guiding light, the glue that holds us together and the air on which we soar. No other part of us knows who we really are, what we really want, and where we really need to be. Until we follow it, every path we take is just another way of getting lost.

Wayne arrived as I finished my summary, appearing in his usual spot beside my desk. I glanced at the clock on my nightstand and then shot him a look. Did heaven go to daylight savings time last night? I quipped.

He smiled, wide at first, then soft and lingering. He placed a hand on the manuscript. His blue eyes glistened in the morning sun.

"I spent my life writing about the miraculous unfolding of the universe," he said. "Now I'm watching you do the same. I just feel thankful. Very thankful."

I felt the same way myself. A month ago, I thought I'd never see him again. Now, he was acting as my private tutor. How lucky was I?

As I looked at him standing in the sunlight, I recounted the various roles he'd played throughout his life: counselor, therapist, professor, writer, lecturer, and actor. It occurred to me that they were all variations of the same primal calling—teacher. Dr. Wayne Dyer had taught in classrooms, in lecture halls, in churches, and in auditoriums. He'd taught on television, on the internet, and on the silver screen. He was still teaching now in the largest venue of all: the afterlife. His physical form had passed, but his light continues to shine.

I thought back to our first class together. How naïve I was, searching for my soul inside myself like it was a set of car keys I'd lost between the cushions of a couch. Our soul is not located within us. What's more, it's not even ours. This explains why so many soul-seekers fail at their quest. They end their search for their soul at the very place their soul begins—at the outer boundaries of their physical form. There is only one soul, and we all share it. Many bulbs but only one light. We can't see this light because we *are* this light. Our soul is not a nightlight we see inside us, it's a spotlight we shine around us. It reveals itself in the peace and joy it manifests in others. That's what heaven is, not an external destination but an internal detonation, an explosion of inner light.

I stopped myself, realizing I was lecturing. Wayne looked at me and smiled.

"Welcome to the light," he said. "How does it feel?"

Wonderful, I answered. Absolutely wonderful.

And it did feel wonderful. More importantly, it felt genuine. For the first time in a long while, there was no countering voice in my head questioning my bliss. I hadn't turned my brain off, not at all. I had merely shown it the light. My mind and soul were no longer in conflict. And I felt complete.

I looked at my spiritual wingman. His eyes were soft and shimmering. He knew our semester was almost finished.

Almost.

"You have one more assignment," he said.

A final exam? I threw up my hands. Sorry, I didn't bring a #2 pencil.

"No," he laughed. "The word for expressing the soul."

I didn't catch his reference at first, then it hit me. The night I lay in bed, trying to think of a word to describe the act of expressing our soul. I recalled the words I'd come up with that night: sensing, knowing, intuiting. They had seemed inadequate then. They seemed even more so now.

"It's a difficult task," he acknowledged. "The soul encompasses many concepts:

"Light—sanctifying, radiating, illuminating.

"Unity—connecting, collaborating, compounding.

"Understanding—intuition, knowing, clairvoyance.

"Power—amplifying, fortifying, inspiring.

"Faith—trusting, welcoming, embracing.

"Appreciation—revering, adoring, exalting.

"Healing—nourishing, revitalizing, comforting.

"Expansion—swelling, sprouting, flourishing.

"It's all these things and more."

Many people would call it God, I said.

"Many people do," he agreed. "But I don't think God is the right word for what you are referring to. Calling the act of being spiritual 'God' is like calling the act of driving 'Chevrolet.' Gods are the vehicles of faith. Spirituality is the road on which they travel. The vehicles are all different, but the road is always the same."

I saw his point. The word God, as used by most religions, was inherently divisive. It assumed that being spiritual required adherence to a particular set of beliefs.

How about praying? I asked.

He nodded tentatively. "That's a good word, but not the right word."

I agreed. Praying was a request for something. Spirituality was giving yourself to others.

What about clarifying?

"I like it," he said. "Seeing through the leaves of your being to the root of your being. You're on the right track."

I thought about a garden. The plants were all different, but the sunlight that sustained them was the same.

Blossoming, I ventured.

"That's a good one too. Human beings respond to love as flowers respond to sunlight."

So is that it? I asked.

"Is what it?"

Blossoming. Is it the right word?

My spiritual wingman shook his head. "You're still trying to make a problem out of this, John. Let it go. The universe is not a problem, therefore it has no solution. It's a miracle that never stops unfolding, an ever-blossoming flower." He motioned toward my box of notes. "This puzzle you've been assembling, you never needed to put it together, you simply needed to stop breaking it apart."

I grabbed my pen, and, in a rush of tinglies, made one final note:

> The puzzle of life is solved when you realize
> it doesn't have any pieces. Everything is one.

"Everything is one," Wayne whispered. And with that, our spiritual semester officially ended. *Soul Understanding 101* was complete.

"You've graduated," he announced with a grin. "Sorry, I don't have a diploma to give you. Enlightenment will have to do."

I turned toward the window, looking out at a world that seemed to sparkle anew, and I thought to myself, *Yes, enlightenment will do quite nicely.*

For a moment, neither of us said anything, then I asked him what the starting salary was for a first-year spiritual guru, and he laughed. When he stopped, I asked him a serious question.

What do I do now?

"You've opened up a new world for yourself. Now go out and live it. As you do, write about it."

I didn't have to ask him if he would be accompanying me on this journey. I think he looked forward to it as much as I did.

A new thought popped into my head. *There are no self-serve fuel pumps in heaven. It's full service or no service at all.* But I didn't write it down. That was a story for a different day. As for today?

I looked at him.

What do we do now?

He shrugged at first, then a playful grin stretched out across his face. He turned toward the window. As he did, the sun crested over the top of the adjacent building, filling the room with dancing columns of light.

"Let's go for a walk."

THE END

AUGUST 29, 2015, LETTER TO WAYNE

Dear Wayne,

I begin this letter by asking if you are surprised to hear from me. I have a feeling you are not. I have a feeling you've been waiting for me to contact you.

If so, what follows won't surprise you. If not, here's my story.

Do you remember the night last September when you told me that my life was going to change in the coming year? Well, it happened, just as you predicted. On December 29 of last year, I woke up at 3:18 a.m. with an idea in my head. *The search for the soul is not a journey but a homecoming*. For some reason, I felt compelled to write it down. In doing so, I seemed to open a floodgate of ideas. Since then, I've written thousands of pages of notes on subjects like love, faith, power, fear, and forgiveness. I'm not sure what is happening to me, and I hope you can shed some light on it. I need your help. I'm flying solo here, and I need a spiritual wingman.

Love,
John

PS. A chill comes over me as I sign this letter. In doing so, I am publicly revealing my shift for the first time. The thought of this both excites and unnerves me. I think I will always remember this day as the turning point in my life. August 29, 2015. The day the new me was born.

I'll call you on my birthday. Talk to you then.

ABOUT THE AUTHOR

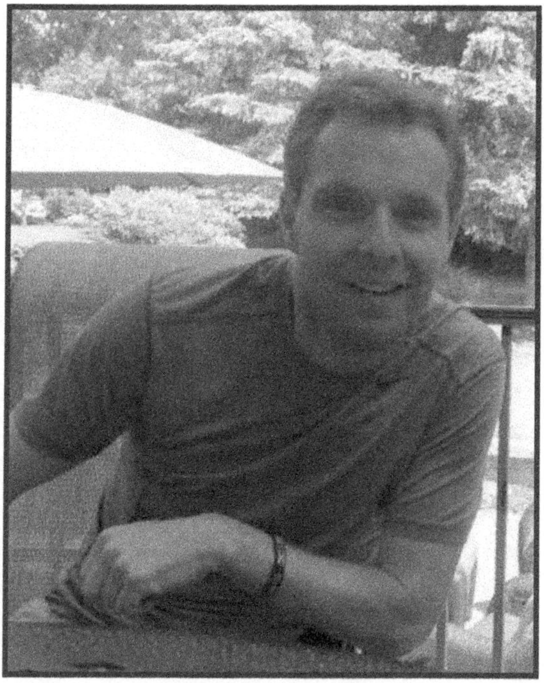

John Dyer is a soul searcher who yearned for a deeper experience of life. *Soul Understanding* is the story of how he discovered that experience, with help from his spiritual wingman, aka Dr. Wayne Dyer. John lives on an island in

Florida where he operates a non-profit homeless shelter for misfit spiritual musings that won't let him sleep through the night.

Soul Understanding is his first book.
To learn more, go to www.loudspirit.com.

www.ingramcontent.com/pod-product-compliance
Lightning Source LLC
LaVergne TN
LVHW041220080426
835508LV00011B/1012
* 9 7 9 8 9 8 6 8 8 4 2 0 2 *